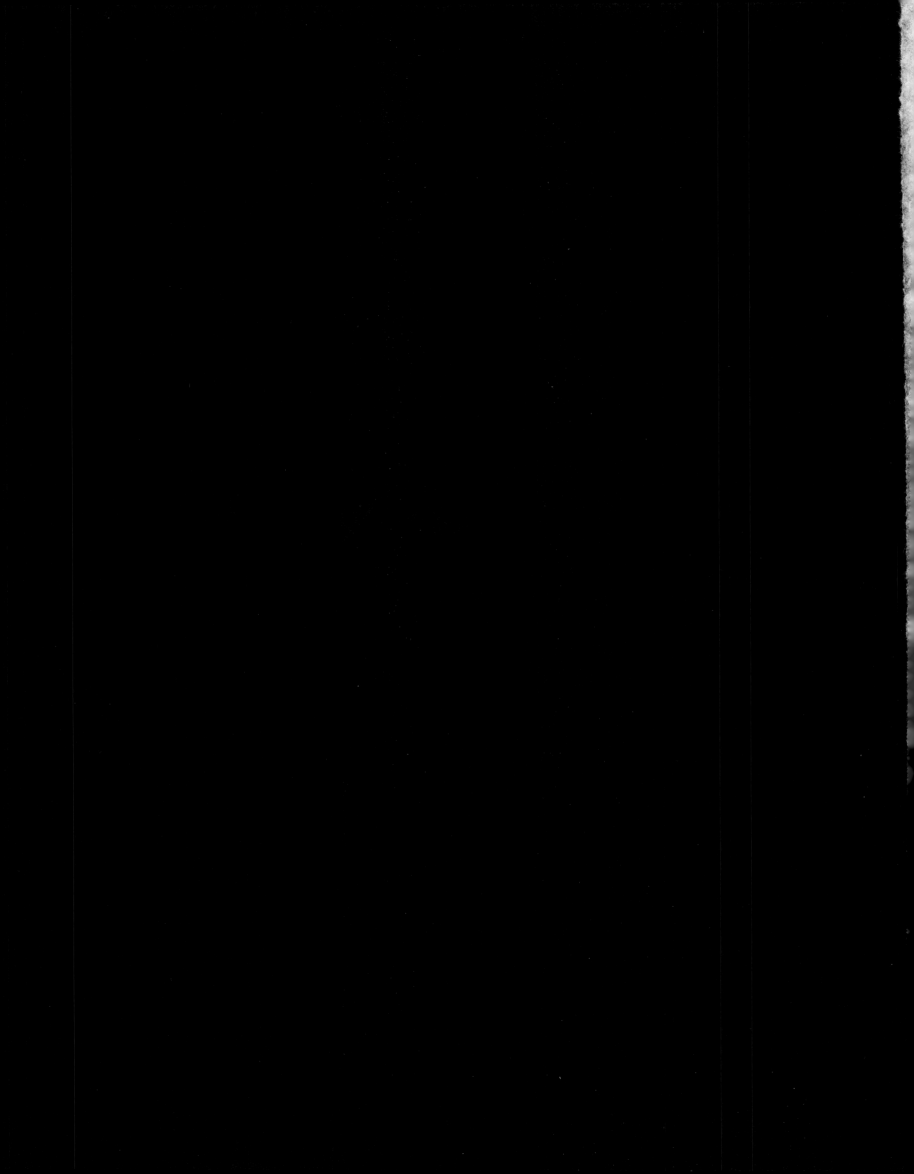

South African Mosaic

TC ROBERTSON SOUTH AFRICAN MOSAIC

C. STRUIK PUBLISHERS
CAPE TOWN
JOHANNESBURG
1978

C. Struik Publishers, 56 Wale Street, Cape Town.

First edition 1978.

Copyright © Text: T.C. Robertson 1978.

ISBN 0 86977 085 3.

Designed by Willem Jordaan, Cape Town.

Lithographic reproduction by Hirt & Carter (Pty) Limited, Cape Town.

Photosetting by McManus Bros (Pty) Limited, Cape Town.

Printed and bound by Printpak (Cape) Limited, Cape Town.

CONTENTS

The spoors of change

Everywhere in South Africa the march of change has left clearly discernible spoors. There are not only the battle-fields of recorded history, marked by forlorn white-painted crosses in the veld, or neglected buildings waiting to become historical monuments, there are fossils, too, the oldest in the world – blue-green algae and bacteria, the beginnings of life.

From the nature of their environment many South Africans have become intensely aware of the succession of natural and man-made events, which from the Earlier Stone Age to the Space Age transformed the landscape in which they live. They can follow the spoors of events on the veld of the great inland plateau, in the Bushveld savannah and even in the groves of forest giants that cower in mountain valleys where they have escaped the axe. The first diamond diggers sifted stone tools out of the terraced river gravels and the steel mouldboard plough tore them from the topsoil of the new maize fields; in a limestone quarry miners' dynamite exposed the fossil skull of a hominid child that played there more than a million years ago; a clay furnace, once stoked with goatskin bellows, has been excavated near where the coke ovens of a steelworks smoke today; and the stone circles stacked round living sites by people of the Uitkomst culture, the first men to use iron weapons and tools in their onslaught on the environment, have given place to the city of Gold – *iGoli*, as the blacks named Johannesburg. To the south, where the first whites came in their wagons, there was a natural wonder as remarkable as the prairies and the pampas – the sweetveld grasslands on which lived the greatest biomass of wild animals in the world. Soon it was fenced and grazed and ploughed under to become Africa's largest granary.

It was almost as if Nature had placed at the feet of those South Africans who could read the signs, strange show-cases of the museum of man as examples of the work of evolution. As a result these people are time-conscious – aware of the matrixes of history that shaped man's past on the once 'Dark Continent' and alert for any signs that the Great Pattern Maker may suddenly be changing the mould into which the superheated stream of contemporary events is poured.

When they look at the teeming niches of their habitat, they are conscious that the stream of life and change is of great variety and complexity, veined with rills and rivulets and flooding or fading with the rains and the droughts. And in their thoughts, as there has always been in the mind of man, there is a constant striving to find a pattern, a grand design, which will enable them to orientate themselves in terms of their total environment and answer the three basic questions of being: 'What am I? Who am I? Where am I going?'

In their recorded history, the series of events from the Age of Navigation to the last quarter of the 20th century, they find numerous causes of change. From them they have selected what they comprehend, according to their time-perspective and culture, to be the main sum of things, a synoptic vision of the process that is shaping their destiny.

This book, too, has been selective – as any account of so vast a panorama of events must be. It sees in the emergence of southern Africa from the past into the laser beams of science and technology three main forces that form a synthesis that can be comprehended by the world community of this age.

At the outset it analyses the influence of man on the five largest ecosystems of the total South African environment which in turn has shaped the work, temperament and migratory movements of the people; and this interaction has been so intricate that it is often difficult to know where one influence ceases and the other begins.

It also probes the psychological driving force, the inner compulsion of man's evolutionary nature, and finds it mainly in the deep-rooted territorial imperative – the land hunger that is shared equally by an expanding white society with private ownership of land and the blacks with communal grazing and small cultivated areas traditionally allocated by chiefs. Then, as now, rapidly growing populations need to be fed.

From a nuclear area around the Great Lakes of the Equator the blacks shifted across the land to find water sources, good soil, lush grazing and village sites to suit their needs. And in all the related cultures that evolved among them there were common elements – the belief in the pervading influence of ancestral spirits on the mortal world and the rituals which this required. In this way the bright cultural tapestry of black Africa was woven and spread since long before the birth of Christ until early in the 18th century when the eastern stream of the black migration had moved south to the Fish River and made contact with whites moving north, and just as hungry for land.

The white migration was small in numbers but moved with big strides from farm to farm. The colonists of the Cape reached this eastern frontier within a century of their crossing into the Overberg, away from the Cape vineyards. Then in 1836 there was a sudden dispersal of about 6 000 Voortrekkers with some thousand wagons into land depopulated in the decade after 1818 by a cataclysmic disaster among the blacks which they called the *Mfecane* – the scattering. In this massacre it is estimated that up to the time of his death in 1824 the *impis* (regiments) of Shaka, the Zulu king, put a million and a half people to death. And into that part of Natal south of the Tugela River which had been almost cleared of inhabitants came the Great Trek in search of its Promised Land.

The pieces of the entire mosaic of peoples north of the Orange River, as they were at the time of the Great Trek, were scattered into a grand design seen as a fist-shaped population vacuum punched in the demographic map by the might of the Zulu war machine and into which the whites trekked. This pattern forms the basis of current socio-political and economic planning.

The third force, perhaps the most powerful of all, is spiritual – the two-way process of acculturation, which began when explorers made contact and missionaries came to seek converts. From language and religion it spread until it pervaded the minds, habits, manners and demands made on the lives of both the blacks and the whites. Soon the use of artefacts needed to develop the new society had to be taught and mastered. Change was speeded up by the growling engine of technology that enabled mines, farms and factories to produce more wealth for a country where the population is now increasing as rapidly as anywhere in the world.

In the turmoil of contemporary events the working of these long-term forces is not easy to detect and measure. All the attention is focused on short-term adjustments such as the provision of work, housing and food – and on the right of all the people to have a say in the making of plans. But the crux of the matter is that the outcome of the efforts to achieve an orderly, prosperous and just society will be decided by the basic design of the South African mosaic – the deterministic, antecedent forces that shaped the complex environment and plurality of cultures that are reflected in this book.

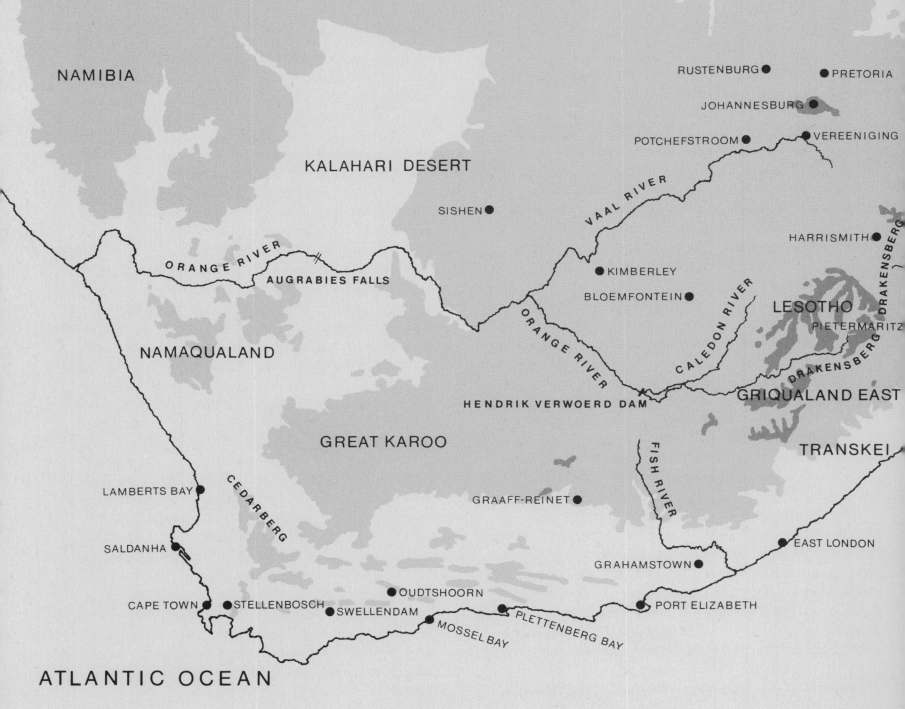

BOTSWANA

NAMIBIA

KALAHARI DESERT

RUSTENBURG ● ● PRETORIA

JOHANNESBURG ●

POTCHEFSTROOM ● ● VEREENIGING

VAAL RIVER

SISHEN ●

HARRISMITH ●

DRAKENSBERG

ORANGE RIVER

AUGRABIES FALLS

KIMBERLEY ●

BLOEMFONTEIN ●

CALEDON RIVER

LESOTHO

PIETERMARITZ

NAMAQUALAND

ORANGE RIVER

DRAKENSBERG

GRIQUALAND EAST

HENDRIK VERWOERD DAM

TRANSKEI

GREAT KAROO

FISH RIVER

LAMBERTS BAY ●

CEDARBERG

GRAAFF-REINET ●

SALDANHA ●

EAST LONDON ●

GRAHAMSTOWN ●

OUDTSHOORN ●

CAPE TOWN ● ● STELLENBOSCH

● SWELLENDAM

PORT ELIZABETH ●

MOSSEL BAY

PLETTENBERG BAY

ATLANTIC OCEAN

RHODESIA

LIMPOPO RIVER

MOZAMBIQUE

OUTPANSBERG
● LOUIS TRICHARDT

PHALABORWA ●

● OHRIGSTAD
● LYDENBURG

LEBOMBO MTS

BARBERTON ●
MAPUTO ● DELAGOA BAY

SWAZILAND

NEWCASTLE
ZULULAND

GELA RIVER

● DURBAN

INDIAN OCEAN

Southern Africa

1 000 – 2 000 m

2 000 m +

SCALE 1: 6 000 000

| 0 | 100 | 200 | 300 kilometres |

| 0 | 100 | 200 miles |

I

A crucible of cultures

The European settlement in South Africa was born on the banks of a small river between an Atlantic Ocean bay and a superb mountain rampart of sandstone and granite, in a landscape that had more of the magnificence of a cathedral nave than the simplicity of a crib. When Commander Jan van Riebeeck's three little Dutch ships dropped anchor shortly after sunset on Saturday the 6th of April 1652, they brought to the outer door of Africa offerings of the Age of Trade and Navigation – trade goods and copper for barter, guns and gunpowder to meet any opposition, seeds and garden tools to work the fertile land, the Bible, and the influence of Calvinism.

The small party that accompanied the founder was made up of humble men who had come to plant a garden. They were not wise men following a star, but in the course of the next three centuries they and their successors did slowly illuminate the Dark Continent with the intellectual and spiritual legacy of their homeland.

Like the rocket trips to the moon of our own day, their voyage had been made possible by courage and technology. The success of the Portuguese in rounding Africa, sailing out of the Atlantic into the Indian Ocean, was the reward they reaped from the inventiveness of their shipwrights who devised a build and rig of sailing vessel that commanded the seas for four centuries. Of its three masts the foremast and mainmast carried square sails, giving driving power; the mizzenmast carried a lateen sail and so the voyagers could sail into the eye of the wind. Unlike the Arab traders down the east coast of Africa, they were not dependent on the direction of the monsoon. Later, the Dutch substituted fore-and-aft sails for the lateen sail on the mizzenmast, with jibs between the foremast and the bowsprit, giving their ships even greater manoeuvrability. The cargo vessels also became warships when, early in the 16th century, they opened port-holes on both sides between-decks to enable a row of guns to fire a broadside. Unlike the mechanically driven modern vessels, only mobile while their fuel lasts, they could keep to the seas for many months on end. The wind might vary, but it was inexhaustible. The only limit to the length of the journey was the food supply – and it was this fact which brought Van Riebeeck with some 90 officers and men to the Cape of Good Hope to produce vegetables and barter beef and mutton from the indigenous brown-skinned Hottentots (Xhoi).

Not all those who sailed in her came as settlers, so the *Drommedaris* has not acquired the almost legendary status that Americans give to the *Mayflower*. It flew the flags of the Amsterdam Chamber of the Dutch East India Company, a signal that it had come to trade and not to colonise or build a nation. But all sailors admire this *pinasschip* as a beautiful example of the work of the 17th century Dutch shipbuilders. It was small, with a deck length of about 90 Amsterdam feet, but the wide forward beam, the graceful almost flamboyant sheer, and the carving finished in natural colours were all characteristic of this period and country. And those she carried must have been all unaware of how great a task awaited them as they crowded on her deck to watch Table Mountain, the splendid portal of the new land, brightly lit in the rays of the sun setting over Signal Hill.

Today, with the perspective of three centuries of history, one can realise the many providential events in the planning of the expedition, the voyage, and the ultimate resolve of some of these Dutchmen to remain at the Cape for good; and one can understand that the Afrikaner has a strong sense of destiny and of Divine purpose and guidance in his emergence and growth to maturity as a nation.

But earlier, in 1647, a gale had blown the Dutch East Indiaman, the *Haarlem,* aground in Table Bay during the rainy season when the ground under the *fynbos* (indigenous vegetation of the Cape) was soft, and the shipwrecked crew, who had saved garden tools and vegetable seeds – cabbages, pumpkins, turnips and onions – were able to reap abundant crops during the six months before they were rescued. They sailed back to Holland with pleasant memories of a fair and fruitful land inhabited by a peaceful indigenous people. Southern Africa had given them her brightest smile of welcome.

On their subsequent report, the directors of the Dutch East India Company in Amsterdam decided to establish a revictualling station on the shores of Table Bay. Nutritional diseases were crippling the crews of ships on the long voyage to the East: indeed, in a sense, scurvy could be considered one of the determinants in the course of South African history. Vasco da Gama had lost no fewer than 100 out of 160 men when he rounded the Cape in 1498.

But in fact there was no need to grow vegetables and fruit at the Cape to prevent deficiency disease. A prophylaxis against

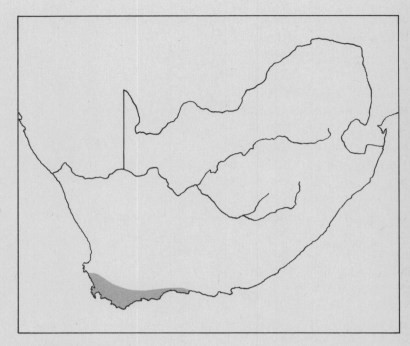

The Western Cape.

scurvy had been known since 1593 when Hawkins made an English ship's company drink lemon juice. In 1776 Captain Cook, with a liberal supply of lemons in the hold, made a voyage of three years and 18 days and lost only one man to this disease, thereby winning the Copley Medal of the Royal Society for 'discovering the means by which under Divine Favour such a voyage can be made'.

The rain clouds that shrouded the mountain and fed the rivulets in the valleys were another such 'Divine Favour'. The *Haarlem* party could clear the proteas and heaths and watch the vegetables grow when the sun shone. Accordingly their report was in the nature of the soil fertility surveys that precede land utilization plans drawn by modern agriculturists when they open new regions for farming. Had the south-east wind grounded their ship during the blistering summer months the soil would have been as Van Riebeeck found it, 'hard as iron', and they would have had to quarry rather than dig their seedbeds.

Even when he was still in Holland, Van Riebeeck had not been optimistic about the Cape venture. He had been there for 18 days in January 1648, in the heart of summer, as a member of the company of the *Coningh van Polen,* which rescued the *Haarlem's* crew; and he had kept his eyes open to observe what kind of people lived in this land. The *Haarlem* report had dismissed it as 'sailor's talk' to describe them as 'a brutal and cannibalistic people, of whom nothing good could be expected'. In his criticism of the report, Van Riebeeck asserted that they could not be trusted at all. He even went so far as to call them 'a brutal lot, living without conscience'.

Fortunately, when the Dutch landed in April 1652, the Hottentots were away on the flats and behind the mountains with their herds. Only Strandlopers, Hottentot food-gatherers who owned no cattle, were left in the intertidal zone. In a few words of broken English one of them, Autushumao, better known as Harry, welcomed them. He had sailed in an English ship to Bantam and acquired a smattering of slang in the fo'c'sle, and so there was no confrontation as there had been in 1509 when 65 of Viceroy d'Almeida's best men were slaughtered when they came ashore to take on fresh water and barter cattle.

After that the Portuguese had given the Cape a wide berth and staged their voyages to sail direct from St. Helena to Mozambique Island. But for this they might have been there on the shores of Table Bay when the Dutch arrived. The Dutchmen might even have found Chinese there, save for one of the strangest quirks of history – and Oriental thinking. Before the inventions of the Portuguese naval architects, the Chinese had the best ships in the world and could conceivably have forestalled the Portuguese in rounding the Cape and might even have anticipated the Spaniards in discovering and conquering the Americas. But after 1433 they discontinued their maritime expeditions, possibly because China's increasing affluence made them unnecessary. It was undoubtedly the poverty of their own countries that stimulated the rulers of Western Europe to encourage overseas enterprises. So colonialism begins with the poor boy setting out to make his fortune, like Dick Whittington going to London – or a global version of the log cabin to White House myth.

Yet the Chinese could have colonised the Cape in quite a different manner by being brought there by the Dutch. When Van Riebeeck saw the Cape flats and sampled the fertile soil in the first river valley behind Devil's Peak, he actually thought that this kind of land could best be developed by industrious Chinese peasants, whose work he had seen when he was trading silk in Taiwan and Japan. He did write to his superiors in Batavia asking for 'een hondert laboreuse Chinesen hujsgesinnen' (a hundred industrious Chinese families), which would have amounted to the West using the East to exploit Africa. Labourers were indeed embarked, but did not sail because of an outbreak of smallpox. Again, one is tempted to ask whether this was just the roll of fortune's dice or the hand of Providence?

Similar speculation applies to the world situation wherever the marauding voyagers of the West made contact with the indigenous peoples of other continents. A good example is the landing of Cortes on the very day in the Mexican prognostic religious calendar that the reincarnation of Quetzalcoatl, the Inca god, was expected. But in South Africa these turns of fortune's wheel are of greater significance because they still influence contemporary thinking and belief in destiny. On the 16th of December of every year the Afrikaner nation observes the Day of the Covenant in obedience to the promise made in 1838 by their devout leader Sarel Cilliers, that if God granted them victory over the Zulus they would build a church in His name and celebrate the anniversary of the deliverance as a day of thanksgiving. But if the Zulus at Blood River had attacked during the dark of night instead of waiting for first light, this decisive battle between white and black in South Africa might have had a different outcome.

A study of the genesis of colonialism reveals how such events shaped a different course for the Portuguese, the Dutch, the British and the French. And for each one the final chapter may have a very different conclusion; there is even the possibility that the history of the Dutch in South Africa, which is still being written, may culminate in a union instead of an estrangement of all the diversity of peoples involved. The Dutch at the outset were fortunate that, unlike the Portuguese who clashed with the Arabs on the east coast of Africa, they did not have to evict a rival on the great trade route. The sporadic resistance from the Hottentots already at the Cape was quite ineffective once the colonists could pursue them on horseback. But the greatest blessing of all was the climate, for they encountered neither malaria nor sleeping sickness. The myth of untold wealth in the interior was the lodestone that drew the Portuguese explorers into the tropical forests and the thornveld savannahs. When it exploded, they left the east coast to the Jesuits and in due course the gardens they planted with so much industry were overgrown with weeds – the pioneers of the jungle's return.

How did this strange new plant at the Cape survive the continent's processes of natural selection, become deep-rooted and in turn spread its seed far and wide? In what mood did those ten peasant families, the first free burghers and real founders of white South Africa, watch the fleet sail for Amsterdam while they returned to their plots along the Liesbeek River?

Their motive was not to get rich, otherwise they would have sailed with Van Riebeeck, a commercially-minded man, who went east to the centres of the spice and silk trade. Nor was it a case of having a good if indolent life, the luilekkerlewe in the land of Cockaigne. They remained in their thatched huts with the sod walls because all around them was the splendour of a unique environment. They had grown to love the country. The mother rock of the sandy soils and silt they tilled had been eroded from rocks that were formed by a great river in the Age of Fishes, the Devonian. With a little of it cupped and crumbled in their hands they could feel and breathe the fertility of the good earth which they were the first to till, while all around was a floral kingdom, a pointillist landscape, in which more than 2 500 species of wild flowers bloomed in spring. In time this became a botanist's paradise, enriching the gardens of the world with cultivated varieties and hybrids. Linnaeus himself wrote to Governor Ryk Tulbagh: 'May you be fully aware of your fortunate lot in being permitted by the Supreme Disposer of events to inhabit, but also to enjoy the sovereign control of that paradise on earth, the Cape of Good Hope, which the Beneficent Creator has enriched with His choicest wonders.' But the paradise was also a haven of peace, securely encircled by the grey ramparts of a mountain range with jagged peaks for parapets.

Indeed, Van Riebeeck and his party had landed in a wilderness area such as Thoreau, the philosopher of Walden Pond in the American forests, or John Muir, climbing the High Sierras, had never dreamed of. But the Dutch also began the process of environmental change which accompanies the gun and the plough and which pioneers boast of as 'taming the wilds'. A few days after their arrival they shot a hippopotamus in the swamp on the Fresh River; they hunted buck on the mountain slopes, wild dogs and civet cats; and when their small flock of sheep was attacked, they joined the Hottentots to hunt the marauding leopard. There was a reward, the price of a cow, for every lion killed by the free burghers. But for more than two centuries the wildlife of South Africa was so abundant that there was no thought that a day would come when it would be endangered, with the quagga and the bloubok extinct and many species only rare survivors on the veld and in the bush.

The beauty of the Cape is different, but well matched by the charm of the other regions into which the white South Africans would migrate – the vastness of the sweetveld *vlaktes*, smaller than the American Great Plains but just as magnificent; the Bushveld, haunted by the spell of man's whole evolutionary past; and the lush coastal forests, just beyond the reach of tropical Africa. As a result they have developed a patriotism not militant and aggressive, but pervaded by an intense and gentle love for their country. The national anthem is not a prayer for a monarch, a call to arms, or the boastful posturing of imperialist might. It is a descriptive lyric, suggestive of the style that began with Milton, and it tells of blue heavens, deep seas, and eternal mountains with krantzes that echo a voice which calls for the people to live or die for their country – a call to which they have often responded courageously.

Every year on the anniversary of the landing, the splendid notes of that anthem resound from the commemorative service held at the statue of Jan van Riebeeck at the foot of a modern city street. Nothing remains of the mountain stream that flowed into the moat of the first fort, or of the jetty down which water barrels were rolled to supply the fleets of Indiamen at anchor in the bay. There are only vestigial traces of the graceful buildings that arose during the first two centuries – fine examples of

Dutch architecture, followed by the English style after they occupied the Cape in 1806, bringing a new culture to impose fresh designs.

The habitat has changed, but the genetic code continues to issue its instructions in defiance of the ideas of social planners. The biological traces of the nomadic Hottentots (Xhoi) are all that remain as witness of their existence. The fact is that for three centuries Cape Town, the Mother City of South Africa, has functioned as a cultural crucible and a pool of genes. History poured into this landscape – the mould fashioned by climate and soil – the ingots of orchards, vineyards and fields of wheat and the ornate white gables of Dutch and French architecture. From Van Riebeeck's wooden jetty in the old harbour there flowed a variety of human blood-lines that can be traced back along the sea lanes to the banks of the Amstel, the Tagus or the Thames; and then East to the Indies and China and beyond that to the Phillipines.

In South Africa custom and policy, often based on biblical precepts, have attempted to keep the blood-lines apart, like a chain of pools in which there is only slow seepage through the restraining marsh soils and reeds. It has been dictated by the fear of a future that could sweep away the pattern and leave the silt-laden turbulence of chaos. But the signs of the natural process are there for all to read. In every one of the city's narrow streets the varied features of the human form reveal the subtle brush-strokes of heredity: slanting oriental eyes smile; a skin like bronze glistens in the sun as a worker strips off his shirt; the blond-and-blue of the Nordic races has left the ships to remain on these shores; and slowly, with the steatopygous wobble of a remote Hottentot ancestor, the washerwoman with a bundle under her arm passes by.

The American melting-pot of races produced a cultural phenomenon. In South Africa differences of skin pigmentation have produced the Cape coloured. But today the old concepts of blood and colour, ingrained in the nation's cultural past, are being modified in the new world where the inhabited land surface, the *Oikounomenê*, is being traversed with the speed of flight and light. The new technology of communication by air travel and satellite pictures projected onto the home television screen is extending contacts and horizons. Its effect will be far greater than those of the Age of Navigation, and South Africa may itself produce a unique cultural phenomenon. And in the process the coloureds are shaking off the chains of traditional restraints and seeking greater freedom in the spheres of political, economic and legislative rights.

The way the indigenous Hottentot tribes changed under the impact of the white man's arrival was mainly due to barter – in order to part them from their animals, they had to be given something in return. When the marginal utility of copper decreased – as the process would be described by modern economists – a more desirable currency was substituted. The Hottentots do not appear to have known how to smoke when the Dutch came to lay out their garden and build their fort. But in the 66 years since Ralph Lane had brought the plant from the West Indies and Sir Walter Raleigh had shown, despite social disapproval, how to smoke the leaves, the Hollander had become used to his long-stemmed clay pipe. From 1652 onwards almost every expedition that set out from the Cape to barter with the Hottentots carried a supply of tobacco as the most valuable article in concluding a deal. The plant did not grow well in the climate of Van Riebeeck's garden, but it thrived later when new immigrants from Europe, the Huguenots, cultivated it at Fransch Hoek. However, the Hottentots did have a pre-tobacco opiate, which the Dutch improved by importing a more potent species from the East. Graevenbroek, who visited the Cape in 1685, described how they powdered the leaves of wild dagga (*Leonotis leonurus*) and made it into cakes about the size of a riksdaalder. They chewed these and also made a decoction of the seeds for headaches and several other ailments. '*Makdagga*' (*Cannabis sativa*), the marijuana of today's drug traffic, was probably introduced during Van Riebeeck's days. In 1704 Kolben commented at length on the fondness of the Hottentots for the '*daggapyp*', which they used to inhale the smoke through water. The Hottentots said that it banished care and anxiety, like wine or brandy, but Kolben saw them raving, staring and capering as if possessed and 'lose themselves in a million of the wildest actions and incoherencies'. This urge for euphoric release makes one wonder if the life of the noble savage was indeed as happy and idyllic as Rousseau depicted it.

And the life of the Hottentots could never be 'free', as a Jet Age traveller imagines himself to be, because they were tied to their herds; and the cattle and hairy sheep were in turn bound to the grasslands and widely-spaced water-points. They had brought domesticated animals with them as they migrated down Africa from a point of origin possibly somewhere in what is now north-west Tanzania. This distinguished them from the Bushmen with whom they became both culturally and racially allied, but who were not pastoral. Among the Hottentots, food-gathering and hunting were important activities of the men while, in contrast with pastoral black tribes, milking was the work of women. But the environment in which they had to keep on the move was hostile. The stock had to be close-herded and kraaled at night for protection against lion, leopard, jackal and wild dog. So the kraal was at the centre of the villages of beehive huts, each dwelling covered with grass mats, which could be loaded on the backs of pack-oxen when the tribe trekked to better pastures or new water-points.

Their ideas of ownership were entirely different from the Roman-Dutch concepts of the colonists. Each family owned its livestock, but groups living together pastured their animals in common. The land belonged to the tribe – and it was prepared to defend its territory against invaders – but no individual, not even the chief, had the exclusive right to any part of it. On the other hand, wild game was considered to be the property of the chief.

About six months after his landing, Van Riebeeck's scouts reported that they had seen the camp fires of a large group of Hottentots moving slowly from the north towards the Cape Peninsula. The supreme test of establishing a *modus vivendi* with the nomads was at hand. The Dutch made ready for the possibility of aggression. The guards were strengthened and they worked furiously to raise the height of the walls of the fort. Hunger was also a factor in the psychological situation because supplies were running low and the colonists knew that it would be months before a fleet could bring relief. The workmen were complaining about their diet of young seals, penguins, fish and sea birds' eggs. Sheep had been stolen and some of the men had even plundered the Company gardens at night. It was a tempting thing for such men with guns to watch thousands of Hottentot cattle grazing round the mountain and within sight of the fort.

But in those spring days of October and November 1652, the conciliatory conduct of the Dutch ensured a peaceful coming together, for a time at least, in spite of the fact that they were building their new settlement on the traditional grazing grounds of the Hottentots. There was an exchange of gifts – among them a wooden box full of cut-tobacco and a few pipes for the chief and his men. Courtesy calls were paid; and then the barter agreement had to be made to determine how much copper wire or plate should be exchanged for the cattle and the sheep. But the craving for tobacco had suddenly gripped the Hottentots and, on the 6th of November, Van Riebeeck recorded in his *Journal:* 'If we had no tobacco there would hardly be any trade, as a whole cow would often be withheld for a finger's length of tobacco or a pipe.'

Only company officials were allowed to trade and the prices they fixed were obviously intended to please their lords and masters of East Indies House in Amsterdam. But Harry, the interpreter, had different and more sophisticated standards of value. Much to the annoyance of Van Riebeeck, he began to intrigue with the chiefs. In the process he earned the distinction of obtaining a South African 'first' in that small group of pioneers round Table Bay – that of the first agitator.

So the Dutch and the Hottentots, although they differed so widely in culture, language and ideas about property, attempted to set up a trading relationship. Much of Van Riebeeck's *Journal* is devoted to an account of the problems of this barter. There were disputes about prices, the shortage of tobacco, and thefts, quarrels and murder. The larger cattle-owning tribes were coming in slowly and men had to be sent out to them to trade. On one hand the possession of cattle and sheep was necessary to ensure the welfare of the tribe and keep it functioning as a social unit; and on the other mutton and beef had to be obtained to fill the larders of the passing ships. Obviously the relationship was unstable and liable to deteriorate.

But the first serious clash in which guns opposed bone-tipped assegais and blood was shed was territorial. The settlement was expanding and by 1659 it covered the present-day areas of Wynberg and Rondebosch, suburbs of Cape Town. This prevented the Hottentots from using the rich grazing at the foot of the mountain. Both the strategy and the tactics of their retaliation were well planned. Instead of risking a frontal attack on the fort, they plundered the Dutch herds at night – especially in wet weather when it was difficult for the Europeans to use their firelocks. When pursuit was attempted the plodding Dutch infantryman was no match for the fleet-footed nomad.

In this 'War with the Cape Clans', as it came to be known, the Europeans made two discoveries – one military and the other geopolitical – which shaped the course of much of their future in southern Africa. The soldiers of the garrison, with reinforcements from a large East Indiaman, could not even make contact with the enemy. But four horsemen, who encountered a party of five Hottentots by accident, killed three of them. Van Riebeeck saw the implications and obtained more horses and some powerful dogs from Java, 'so that the Europeans now felt themselves more than a match for a legion of Hottentots'. And yet it is doubtful whether they were able to put into the field more than 30 mounted men: the prototype of the hard-riding, sharp-shooting South African commando – 'die Boer met sy perd en sy roer' (the Boer with his horse and his gun) – which grew in efficiency and skill to challenge the might of the British Empire, and disappeared only when the armoured car and tank began to rumble over the veld.

The second lesson Van Riebeeck learned from the war with the indigenous peoples was that a geographical boundary was essential to separate the intricate pieces of the human mosaic. In the absence of a suitable river or mountain range he thought of the hedges with which German and Dutch barons indicated their jurisdiction over land.

Part of the food economy of the Hottentots was the bitter almond tree (Brabeium stellatifolium), the fruits of which they peeled, dried and roasted to destroy the toxicity (which once cost a Hollander his life when he tried to eat them straight off the tree). The value of this dangerous almond to the Hottentots was that it could be picked, treated and kept for use back in the arid grazing lands, where the soil was hard and roots difficult to dig up. Van Riebeeck considered it an ideal plant for a hedge and seed-collecting began in 1660, eight years after the first

attempts to establish a friendly, non-territorial relationship based on barter agreements. The green line of this living barrier would go down from the mountains to near the sea.

By the time he left in April 1662, the hedge was growing well; mounted men patrolled between the wooden watch-houses that had been built at intervals along it, and it remained a bitter symbol of proprietory rights and the only formal geographical frontier of the Colony until 1798 when the Great Fish River was proclaimed the eastern boundary.

During Van Riebeeck's time – and even more so under the two Van der Stels – a prodigious amount of work was done. Nothing to equal it was taking place in the tropics; but it may well be that the more temperate climate encouraged the natural energy of the Dutch to extend their arable lands into the distant valleys. Experimental crops, such as the hop, were still being tried out, but after the arrival of the Huguenots, some 176 in all, a definite agricultural system, based on the vine and deciduous fruit, began to develop and persists to this day. Their arrival added a new and vital dimension to the white society being formed at the Cape, for the Huguenots were an industrious and enlightened people. They had fled religious persecution in France and from Holland they emigrated to the Cape and settled in the fertile valleys of what is today the Boland. From the start they intermarried with the local Dutch, adopted their language and forged an identity linked to the land. Theirs was a labour-intensive industry in which the Hottentots could not be induced to take part, although they allowed women and children to go into domestic service. But the men clung to the remnants of their herds, bartering a beast or two only to satisfy a craving for tobacco, and later for liquor.

The Dutch had never contemplated the enslavement of the Hottentots, and until 1658 only ten or 12 slaves from Madagascar and Batavia had been working for the Company. Then an Indiaman arrived with 170 captives, in a miserable condition, taken from a Portuguese slaver bound from Angola to Brazil. Then another shipload, bought by the officers at Popo, arrived with more slaves than the Company needed, so 89 were sold on credit to the burghers. It was formally decreed that they were to be taught the doctrines of Christianity, at a time when less distinction was made between black men and white than between professing Christians and heathens.

There are statistics to show what was happening to the environment and the people of the Peninsula after almost 50 years of occupation by the Europeans. In 1691 there were almost a thousand colonists and they owned 285 men slaves, 57 women slaves, and 44 slave children; 261 horses, 4 198 head of horned cattle, 49 703 sheep and 220 goats. They had 584 950 vines bearing, and had harvested in the last season 4 181 muids of wheat, 808 muids of rye, and 202 muids of barley (1 muid was roughly equivalent to 54 kilograms).

For the next 150 years the main ecological feature of man's relationship to his natural environment at the Cape was the building up and extension of that agricultural and horticultural pattern. The forests were disappearing to become rafters, floors, doors and furniture in the stately farmhouses; the proteas and heaths of the *fynbos* were giving way to orderly vineyards, orchards and fields of wheat. In this calm setting a multiplicity of customs and manners, beliefs and hopes, languages, skills and occupations blended into behaviour patterns that were gaining the acceptance of the whole community: and the crucible is still at work and boiling. Taken together, the landscape and its people form a unique social phenomenon in Africa, and it has come to be known, sometimes somewhat deprecatingly, as Cape culture.

These people of the Peninsula were basically agriculturists, tillers of the soil, with an admixture of craftsmanship that made and maintained the implements they used and brought beauty to their homes. Indeed, most of those who came to sneer at this lifestyle were the product of a social and economic throwback — a return to herdsmanship in the new frontier areas. In the early years of the settlement cattle trade with the Hottentots was a Company monopoly; Van der Stel had threatened anyone who bartered cattle from locals with whipping, branding, banishment and confiscation of property. But on the 27th July 1699, the directors of the Dutch East India Company, who met in Amsterdam and had little idea of what was going on at Groen Kloof where the longhorns were grazing, decided to throw the cattle trade wide open. This must have caused as much excitement as the announcements in the 1960s stock exchange boom that a prosperous private company was 'going public'. The colonists climbed in under very favourable conditions. They were given land for grazing and when the pastures failed, they moved on over the *berg* (mountains), along trails where herds of eland had once migrated, to seek better places to pasture their cattle.

This was the beginning of a kind of streamlined, 18th-century nomadism, equipped with three essential new tools to master the more hostile, summer rainfall regions — wagons instead of grass huts, guns instead of wooden spears, and horses to give the mobility needed for hunting and scouting for water and grazing. As the movement went east, inland from the forest belt along the Indian Ocean's shores, the new Hottentot tribes encountered offered no resistance and there was little evidence of the ultimate territorial challenge — confrontation with the more warlike black peoples. But these cattle farmers from the Cape, who had broken their links with the avenues of oaks, the vineyards and the wheatfields, were the raw material from which would be moulded the basic types of the northern Afrikaner of the future — of the *grensboer* (border farmer), the *trekboer*, who ignored defined boundaries and took his herds

for summer grazing into the plateau grasslands; of the Voortrekkers themselves, and ultimately of the burghers who ruled the impoverished republics of the Transvaal and Orange Free State until the discovery of gold introduced the age of mining and industry.

Meanwhile the agriculturists of the Peninsula relaxed in their benevolent climate and relied more and more on others to do their work for them. By 1795 the number of slaves had increased to 18 000; the importation of Malays both added to the pool of genes and supplied skilled labour.

The Hottentots, with a distinctive cultural pattern of their own, were fading from the scene. The gun had been used against them, but never for mass slaughter as it had been elsewhere in the world. There is no Rattlesnake Buttes in the history of South Africa during the first stages of territorial expansion. The tragedy of the Hottentots was etched rather with a bio-sociological needle. They were first scourged by smallpox when the virus came to the Cape in 1713, carried by dirty clothes from an Indiaman to wash-house slaves, to the town and across the mountains. For a great distance inland the tribes were blotted out by the disease. With their feuds and rivalries and internal wars, they disappeared as organised communities and left only a few broken-spirited and scattered remnants.

But years earlier already, the craving for the euphoria of tobacco and dagga had been indirectly breaking down the traditional tribal structure of the nomads. When the last that remained had no more cattle to barter or land to live on, they had to sell their labour; and so the new nomadism, the 'trek to look for work' began across the mountain passes to the farms and villages. It became part of the economic system of the territory and one of the most important factors in contemporary South African history, for it now includes not just a few sickly Hottentots but millions of blacks who comprise a virile and productive labour force.

Once the major element in the original population of the Cape, the Hottentots have through intermarriage left only the trail of their genes, some words of their language and the ghosts of strange beliefs and customs that walk the back streets of the beautiful Mother City.

But Cape Town is not only beautiful, it is peaceful — a city that for the most part has known little of the ravages of war or revolution. Its chief monuments are to builders, Van Riebeeck and Rhodes, the Huguenots and the founders of the Afrikaans language in the distant valleys. An equestrian statue of General Louis Botha is an almost incongruous reminder in bronze of the human strife and bloodshed of the north; and the image of Jan Smuts sits brooding in the Gardens as if puzzled by the work of hands that would not heed his holism. For all around him there is a human society in which the whole is so obviously greater than the sum total of the varied parts. It is the double helix which was one of the biological blueprints of a new nation. It is still the crucible that is pouring ingots of art and literature, of moral codes and startling hypotheses to be tested by the many social and political experiments that have to be made in Africa before the mosaic of peoples falls into place.

2

The Great Karoo

When they moved over the mountains into the Little Karoo and eastwards along the fringes of the Great Karoo itself, the way of life of the European cattle farmers began to change. They now had to adapt themselves to a country where the rains came irregularly, like dramatic episodes in the course of the seasons. Such conditions dispersed the wagons and herds, with their advance guards of hunters, until they were like a mobile frontier, slowly eating its way into a new land. What the farmers looked for and prayed for most anxiously was a permanent, natural source of water – a stream, a fountain, or a deep hippo pool that would not dry up during the worst drought. Until they had 'found water', they could not settle and build a house, no matter how sweet the grazing might be.

The Karoo is a tableland, which long ago the Bushmen in small bands scoured for succulent herbs and grass. The rains and droughts moved the huge game herds like pieces on a chessboard. There could be the bounty of millions of migrating springbok crossing the flats from the Kalahari, a true desert, or only a few emaciated quagga, black wildebeest and blesbok coming to drink at the mud puddles where the hunters lay in wait with their poisoned arrows.

The landscape, wrinkled with the erosion scars of great age, has features which give it as great a claim to fame as the steppes of Europe, the prairies and pampas of North and South America. In its rocks there is the fossil record of the life form's slow transition from reptile to mammal and the movement of the drifting continents themselves.

In size it is just over a third of the whole of South Africa and the nature of its climate and vegetation has had a profound effect on the development of the country. The first travellers in this semi-arid region to report on its challenge were the explorers; famous men such as Ensign Schryver (1689), Ensign August Beutler (1752) and the plant collectors Dr Anders Sparrman (1772), Carl Thunberg – the 'father of South African botany' – and Francis Mason who sent seeds to be propagated at Kew Gardens in England.

For the men who drove cattle and lived in wagons, the oval Karoo that lay right across the country was a more effective barrier to migratory movement than a sea that could be crossed by ships. So settlement and development took place mainly in the 'Blue Triangle', the heartland of South Africa, where the rainfall is more than 375 millimetres a year. Even the dogs of war did not prowl the Karoo. The battles of tribes and nations and empires were fought round its periphery where the wealth lay – good grazing, flowing rivers, diamonds and gold. Until the flocks of merino sheep, animals well-adapted to the semi-desert conditions, arrived there, the Karoo was a remote, forgotten vastness.

Before the *trekboere* gradually penetrated the landscape, it had already been faintly lined by the traditional paths followed by the Hottentots with their flocks and herds. The southern part of the Karoo had been gently folded in distant geological times by the advance ripples of the fold-storm which built the Cape Mountains. Here the paths went down the steep kloofs that linked the valleys. But once they reached the arid plateau itself, the herds had often struck out arrow-straight across the plains to the water-hole. These paths guided the *trekboere* as they moved away from the almond hedges and memories of the Peninsula.

They had crossed the plains of Camdeboo and were at the foot of the Sneeuberg when Hendrik Swellengrebel, whose father had been Governor of the Cape, arrived there with his expedition in 1776. His description gave a dismal picture of conditions. 'Most of them,' he wrote in his journal, 'now live not much better than the Hottentots.' They paid the rent for their farms to the Company with oxen; they sowed a little wheat for their own use; their houses were four walls of clay, one and a half metres high, covered with reeds; there was no chimney and the floors were made of clay and dung. The contents of the huts were a confusion of butter churns, freshly slaughtered meat and . a menagerie of hens, ducks and piglets. There were practically no slaves, and the Hottentot servants, paid in cattle, only contributed to the disorder. In these little shelters they made butter and soap, and once in a while a wagon-load was taken to the Cape. The families inevitably spent more time in the tents of the wagons than they did under the thatch of a house. In the course of time the wagon became so intimately associated with the evolution of the Afrikaner nation that the intense nationalism, which flared up in 1936, was accompanied by what can only be described as 'the adoration of the ox wagon'. The huts also acquired symbolic significance as they evolved into the *hartbeeshuis* (reed and daub house) with slightly better thatch, a chimney, a double, stable-type door and boarded windows. It was the birthplace of many Voortrekker leaders and also of Paul Kruger. But in the Cape it was the more elegant Dutch *H-huis* in which the cradles of the future leaders were rocked.

These people were also the cultural ancestors of the *grensboere* (border farmers) and of the Voortrekkers themselves. But when Swellengrebel visited them, 60 years before the Great Trek crossed the Orange River, he failed to see the embryo of nationhood in those primitive farms scattered along the edge of the Great Karoo, just inland from the coastal forest belt. Indeed, he prophesied that 'these people, who from their earliest days love to live by hunting in the veld, will wholly sink back into savagery'. The aristocratic young Hollander could not have stuck his nose into the huts of the peasants in Europe, many of whom lived in no better conditions. Indeed, countless slum dwellers of the Industrial Revolution were far worse off than these resolute frontiersmen and women, their spirit tempered by their tough life. And of all the hardships they had to endure, the frequent raids and attacks of the Bushmen were the worst.

The Hottentots and blacks were just as determined as the *trekboere* to exterminate the Bushmen 'vermin'. It was a fierce, aggressive drive – as old as the factors of natural selection that shaped the course of human evolution and produced the 'warrior virtues' of men. Boer, black man and Hottentot had this in common: their cultures were closely bound up with cattle. So those with domesticated animals united to destroy the hunters and food-gatherers of the Great Karoo; and the killings that resulted are one of the most tragic chapters in the history of this harsh environment. Commandos – mounted patrols of farmers armed with heavy muzzle-loaders – spattered the Bushman paintings on the cave sandstone with the blood of the little artists, while the feeble counter-attack, flights of poison-tipped reed arrows, came sailing through the smoke and dust.

When they first moved away from the Cape to the valley farms, the Dutch could not distinguish between the Hottentots and the Bushmen, who looked so much alike. Indeed, it seems that from Stone Age times the same physical type had produced different cultures, just as today there is the same wide range of cultural diversity among the European races. Early travellers to the eastern frontier, learned and well-informed men like Anders Sparrman and Robert Gordon, referred to the Bushmen as the *Kleyne Chineesen* (Little Chinese) or *Snese-Hottentots* (Chinese Hottentots). But irrespective of what Colonel Gordon may have called them, he still regarded the Bushmen as 'little better than baboons'. He would have been amazed indeed at the findings of 20th century anthropological research into the religion and morality of the little clans of hunters. At the time of his famous journeys to the Orange River, Gordon described the Bushmen as 'shyer than any wild animal'. He was with Governor van Plettenberg when the Bushmen refused to come near the long train of wagons to parley and negotiate a peace, although such ideas do not appear to have been beyond their

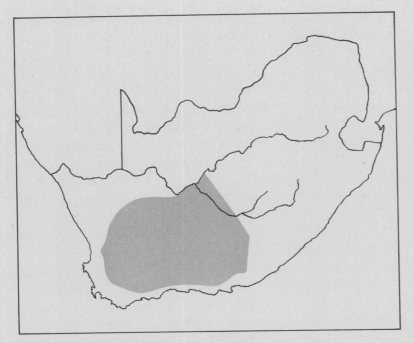

The Great Karoo.

never completely exterminated and some of the clans that escaped into the Kalahari desert are still intact social units, the subject of detailed study as an example of how man whose technology is in the Neolithic stage of development lived with his natural environment.

But the elimination of the Bushman as a predator on the herds and flocks did not open the whole of the Karoo to the farmers. It required a technological change in agriculture and a number of new machines before the great flocks of merino sheep came to graze down the sweet grasses and leave the succulent plants in their place. That change was the creation of artificial water-points – small dams made possible by the arrival of more efficient steel ploughs and the scraper to pile up a wall. Then jumper drills began to sink boreholes in suitable geological formations. Underground water was exploited with increasing efficiency as shot drills went deeper into harder rock, often into centuries-old fossil supplies. But the biggest advance came with the windmills and the thump of their plunger pumps became a familiar sound in later years round the houses of the sheep farmers, now no longer bound to the water-holes where the Bushmen had once lurked with their poisoned arrows.

The Company had imported rams from Persia and Spain to cross with the hairy sheep of the Hottentots. But the wool industry, which was based on the merino sheep, only began to prosper when the English 1820 Settlers brought the expertise needed for the handling of these more delicate animals. One of the most able of these wool pioneers was Lieutenant Richard Daniell, who had built up an efficient unit by 1835 and was making full use of both the Hottentots and local black tribesmen as shepherds and shearers.

The industry spread into the Karoo and encountered an even more dangerous predator than the Bushman – the black-backed jackal (*Canis mesomelas*), a yellow-rufous killer, weighing less than 14 kilograms. Over its shoulders and along its back it had a black-and-white saddle, like a jungle fighter's camouflage cloak. No flocks, and especially no young lambs, were safe from its snapping, snarling flank attacks. It left far more lasting spoors than the Bushmen on the Karoo landscape and its people. Shepherds watched the grazing flocks by day, but at night every sheep had to be within the stone-walled kraal. In their to-and-fro movement from the veld to the kraals, the animals, walking single file, trod footpaths that gathered storm water to become the dongas of soil erosion – a lethal threat to the soil and the farmers' grazing. Mounted hunters with packs of dogs failed to exterminate the jackal, and as recently as 1958 they still shot and trapped as many as 16 000 of the four-legged vermin in a single year.

It was only when the British and German steel industries around 1862 began to mass-produce wire mesh that the Karoo could be paddocked and made safe for the sheep. The farms

comprehension. Their 'wildness' might be explained by their experience with the force under Adriaan van Jaarsveld in 1775 who misled them with a false show of friendship and then killed 180 of them.

Human ecologists have now attempted to explain this cruel and violent clash with the Bushmen in terms of territorialism; the conflict between a food-gathering band which identifies itself very closely with its environment and others who do not share this concept of the natural universe. For instance, while members of a band hunt and collect food freely over their own territory, they are as careful not to trespass as they would be to avoid trampling on the bodies of their neighbours. Indeed, their land, its food and wildlife are regarded as a part of themselves, and an invasion of it is a direct, personal injury – and this was only one of the many sources of mistrust between the Bushmen and the other peoples who invaded their territory.

The herdsmen and the hunters placed identical value on the same kind of land – the area around a permanent water-point or on the banks of a river. Here the Bushmen obtained the highest yield from the pits they dug to trap anything from a hippopotamus or an eland to a springbok or a duiker. Here the farmers, too, had to water their stock every day even if they grazed and kraaled them some distance away. These *suipings* (drinking places) were like oases in the vastness of the semi-arid Karoo and the hills around them, up into the peaks of the Drakensberg where the Bushmen made their last stand in a brave, defiant, death-before-surrender encounter. They were

were now divided into jackal-proof camps that give the 'civilised' Karoo landscape, the centre of South Africa's wool industry, its curiously cubist effect. But the ecological effects of bringing close-cropping sheep into grasslands, where free-roaming herds of game had established a natural balance, have not yet been overcome. Today desert encroachment has become the most dangerous predator of all.

The people of the Karoo have the wide-open-spaces outlook of farmers who must own large tracts of land to make a living. But they are a distinct type, quite different from the cattle rancher. In their natures there is something of the serenity of the biblical shepherd. The area that they graze is the largest agro-economic unit in the Republic of South Africa, bigger than Oklahoma and Kansas put together. Among these farmers, who often cannot see the smoke from a neighbour's kitchen on the horizon, there is little fear that the exploding black population in the high-rainfall areas along the Indian Ocean coastline will crowd their remote *vlaktes* (plains). The future seems to be bound up inextricably with the fate of wool and its rivalry with artificial fibres; for if science can make and mass produce a perfect replica of the complex molecule of wool, the beautiful merinos of the stud farms will have been bred in vain. What gave the world its first portrait of 'an African farm' in the famous novel by Olive Schreiner, may become a different kind of place, where memories of the game herds, the jackals and the little people that would not be tamed will fade entirely and only the advancing desert and the need to find a new way of life will remain realities.

3

The Green Coast

The gradual migration of the black man down Africa was the most important human event on the old continent since the beginning of the Iron Age. It was in the nature of a prehistoric population explosion and the ingredients of the charge that set it off included the hoe and the cultivation of new food crops; food storage in pits and grass baskets; collective hunting of game; herds of domesticated animals; the knowledge that the ash of trees restored some fertility to the soil; and the use of such weapons and tools as the assegai and the axe, baskets and plaited ropes to hold down thatch grass, and a variety of skilfully made and sometimes ornate pottery utensils. In other words, a more effective exploitation of the natural environment provided the food supply required to increase the birth rate and sustain the population that survived disease and the bloodshed of territorial aggression.

This great migration is all the more remarkable since it took place without the wheel, the plough or the horse: these peoples even lacked the knowledge of writing to pass on commands, keep records and transmit knowledge from one generation to the next.

A history book cliche sums up our knowledge of the black man's origin and wanderings – both are said to be 'shrouded in mystery'. Archaeologists, anthropologists and ethnographers have tried to unravel its threads, without complete success. The study of blood groups and skull measurements has revealed no somatic black type, although it is accepted that the criteria of race should be physical, not cultural. The way their craftsmen made things, from clay pots to canoes, was no more revealing. The best clues were provided by the basic vocabulary and structure of the languages of the widely dispersed tribes. Researchers attempted to discover the original Bantu tongue, and from this ur-Bantu it has been deduced that the first clans or tribes kept cattle not sheep, cultivated the soil, used canoes, had the idea of taboo and believed in ghosts. All that the scientific evidence actually indicates is continual movement among the people of Africa for the past 4 000 years, resulting in the transmission of ideas and cultures and the growth of new languages that are only distantly related.

As they moved south they adapted themselves to a great diversity of bioclimatic regions – tropical rain forests and lake shores, vast savannahs that faded away into desert wastes, and the sub-tropical bush of the east coast of Africa. This is the frost-free 'Green Coast' that gets its high rainfall from the warm Mozambique Current, flowing south from the Equator in the Indian Ocean. The northerly movement of peoples was limited by what used to be called the 'Bantu-line' – a linguistic boundary from coast to coast, from the mouth of the Rio dos Reis to Mombasa. A 1945 population estimate put the number of Bantu-speaking people south of that line at 40 000 000; and to the north, in a smaller and more fertile area, there was an equal number of other closely-related black peoples. Numerically they were and remain the dominant force south of the Sahara Desert – the natural barrier to northward movement.

The diversity of the African environment resulted in the blacks forming groups and tribal clusters. The first and most lasting contact of the northwards-moving Europeans of southern Africa was with the large Nguni group, which included the Zulu of Natal, the Swazi and the Matabele of the Western Transvaal and later Rhodesia. The advance guard, which had pushed furthest down the Green Coast, included what were referred to in early reports as the 'Kaffir tribes' of the Transkei – the Xhosa, Thembu and Pondo and refugees from Shaka's reign of terror, such as the Fingoes and the Bhaca. There was little true nomadism in the shift of both the black and the white peoples. It was a slow movement dictated by agricultural needs, or by external and internal political and social pressures.

As they came south from somewhere near the Great Lakes, the cattle-owning Nguni had to follow a general route which was free from the menace of the tsetse fly.

It seems that the three foundation types of African cattle were the Hamitic longhorn, the oldest African bovine, the *Brachyceros,* a dwarf shorthorn from Asia, and the humped Zebu, which came more recently from Asia. Just as the tribes had been formed from a mixture of Hamitic, Negro and Bushman blood, so the herds of cattle developed many regional types from the three basic species.

The proud Zulu of older times even practised the custom of 'horn training' in which they trained the horns of their cattle to resemble those of antelope – the spirals of the kudu or the sharp-pointed horns of the bushbuck ram. They sought uniformity of colour among the herds, and the chiefs were especially proud of those animals that were entirely one colour.

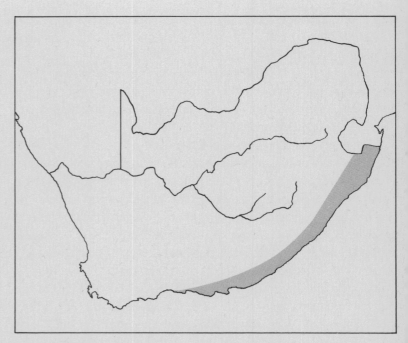

The Green Coast.

Shaka, founder of the Zulu nation, had his *iziTulu* herd of black cattle which Dingane inherited, and the famous all-whites, the *iNyoni-ka-yi-Pumule.* The name means 'the bird will not rest' and it was derived from the chief's boast that he would have so many of these animals that the white cattle egrets, which followed them, would be continually on the move. The milk yield was poor, but rich in cream; and milking was more of a ritual than a practical, economic procedure. In fact ritual and cattle were closely linked; every burial and marriage was accompanied by the ceremonial slaughter of an ox. Their regard for their ancestors and the near-veneration of their cattle were central to their beliefs.

But what was to become a factor of extreme geopolitical importance was the Zulu herdsmen's knowledge of the quality of the grazing. They knew all the areas where the herds put on most weight, where the spring flush of green would first appear and where the sward would last longest. These pastures were the most frequent causes of tribal clashes and even of wars with the white man.

However, it is wrong to regard the Nguni as being no more than hunting-pastoralists. Agriculture made it possible for their numbers to grow and their method of tilling the soil made it necessary for them to keep on the move down Africa because they had to follow the bush and the forest of the Green Coast. Their practice, known as shifting cultivation, was to burn down the trees and hoe in the ashes. In this way the vegetation also determined the population density. Where the forest was

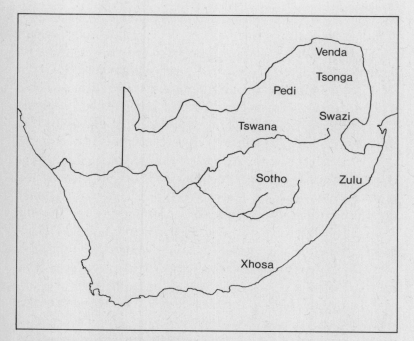

The black peoples of South Africa.

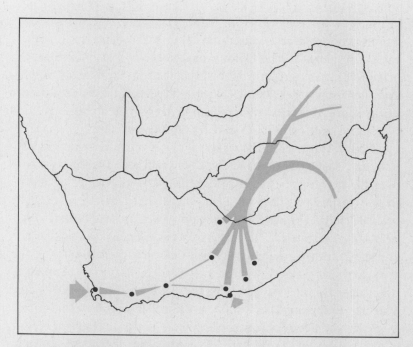

The spread of the white man.

dense, people were able to live permanently in villages and cultivate the surrounding plots in rotation. In lower rainfall areas, which thinned out to become parkland or savannah, they had to move their villages to provide fresh ashes. But the decisive factor was the proportion of resting years to cropping years— the time it would take for the forest or bush to come back once the women with their hoes stopped working the soil because its yield had become uneconomic. This period varied from three years to infinity. Wherever there are blacks, from the Sudan to Nigeria and down to the Transkei, shifting cultivation is still to be found: and its ecological consequence is widespread soil erosion, and a continuous demand for new land.

By the time the moving mass of blacks had sent a 'horn' down the east coast, the need had arisen to establish a border stronger than Van Riebeeck's hedge of wild almond. It was now vital to define and stabilise a zone of contact between the blacks and the *grensboere* – a more settled generation of the *trekboer*. These new border farmers were soon to acquire the farming skills and knowledge brought by the 1820 Settlers.

The hostility of the blacks flared up when they encountered this white-skinned race of cattle-owners and there ensued a long struggle for the possession of the natural resources that both needed – water, grass and soil. By 1812 Governor Cradock had already made the first attempt to keep white and black apart by driving the migration from the north back across the Fish River and building a line of blockhouses – ineffective as they proved. Beyond Van Riebeeck's hedge the Hottentots in the course of

time became fewer and more feeble. But behind every border on the Eastern Frontier the blacks were becoming stronger and more numerous despite their tribal wars.

As commandos of rugged *grensboere* rode out on retaliatory and punitive expeditions and one war followed another, the British at first attempted to stabilise the situation by entering into treaties with the black chiefs, who had little experience of the ethics and implications of this particular form of European statecraft. Indeed, the British have been strongly criticised for assuming that the chiefs appreciated these implications in the same way as the Indian Rajahs or Nawab. But the treaties do represent an attempt to formalise the relationship between black and white.

In 1830 Sir Lowry Cole, the English Governor, gave more precise form to the Treaty System by a decree that every attempt of the blacks to plunder the farms of the *grensboere* would be followed by the immediate expulsion of the whole tribe to which the plunderers belonged. From 1836 to 1844 treaties were entered into with no fewer than ten chiefs; but the herds remained pawns that were taken too easily from both sides of the border by bold raiders who loved cattle and by herdsmen whose customs centred on the cattle kraal and the wealth which it represented.

Land hunger was stimulated by economic growth pains, too. Millions of vines were planted, while the wheat farmers with better ploughs from British factories increased the size of their fields. Between 1806 and 1820 there was a sixfold increase in imports and exports from Table Bay. Even on the remote frontier the *grensboere* sensed the coming of prosperity. Indeed, the cattle herds in the Colony had trebled in size during the period of export growth. But the men of the border areas felt that their hopes were being frustrated by regiments of redcoats using more pipe-clay than gunpowder, by a change in the system of land ownership and by labour problems.

During this period the *trekgees*, the wanderlust that grips a man and makes him yearn for open veld and better pastures over the horizon, began to affect the *grensboere* more strongly than ever before. They sent out small, hard-riding patrols to make surveys of the north, where only the elephant hunters had hitherto penetrated. Their leaders were experienced cattlemen and they ventured as far as the banks of the Tugela River, which was in roaring flood so that they had to shout to exchange greetings and information with the Zulu on the opposite side. Patrols, following the wagon tracks of a new generation of *trekboere*, also rode across the Highveld plains to the Vaal River – the border of Mzilikazi's country. The information they brought back about the climate, the grazing and the water supplies created an image of a new Land of Canaan; and years later, when Gert Maritz's party reached the top of the Drakensberg and looked down into Natal, his people were to cry out: 'This is the Promised Land!'

But the Great Trek was more than a speeding up of the outward movement, the quest for *Lebensraum*, which had been in progress for a hundred years since the earliest wagons cut the spoors and the *hartbeeshuise* were shifted from one water-hole to the next. This time the change of habitat was more deliberate and planned – it was a more organised movement, not the slow migration of family parties, but a long train of wagons that, with each turn of the wheel and step of the oxen, marked the beginning of a new nation. Its psychological impetus came in 1835 from failure and defeat, from the ineffective political and military system of border control, followed by the decision of the British Government to disallow the annexation of land taken from the blacks in war. For the Voortrekkers, as they came to be known, driving a spearhead towards Natal into the tribes between the Drakensberg and the sea now seemed to be ruled out. The strategy would be an outflanking movement by trekking north across the Highveld plateau and then east down the mountains. Moreover, there was a belief that the route had been mapped by Divine destiny and this gave the Afrikaners of the Highveld *vlaktes* and the malarial bush country their Genesis and Exodus. The battles they fought from their *laagers* and the tribulations of the trail endowed them, and the next three generations, with a tradition of courage and endurance. A hundred years later, on a *kopje* overlooking a new capital city, Pretoria, they would be able to build a Hall of Fame to symbolize the tragedy and the glory of the Trek, with the statues of their heroes who had sought freedom in the wilderness.

But the problems of the border – the confrontation of Nguni with Boer and Briton – were not solved when the wagons set off towards the Orange River drifts. Twelve years later Governor Sir Harry Smith, the dashing Peninsular veteran and Indian soldier, decided to annex the territory between the Keiskama and the Kei Rivers to Britain, not the Cape, and he named it British Kaffraria. The chiefs were given orders that were in the nature of Eleven Commandments. They were to: 1. obey the laws; 2. compel others to do the same; 3. stop witchcraft; 4. prevent the violation of women; 5. abhor murder; 6. make their people honest and peaceable and not rob the Colony; 7. acknowledge that they held their lands from the Queen; 8. recognise the Queen as their only chief; 9. stop buying wives; 10. listen to the missionaries; 11. bring a fat ox every year for the Queen.

To warn the chiefs of the consequences of disobedience, Sir Harry put on a show that must have been one of the most bizarre demonstrations of menace in the history of the settlement of territorial disputes. At his command a charge of gunpowder blew one of his wagons to smithereens. And that, he told the chiefs, would be their fate if they disobeyed. Then he tore up a sheet of paper and threw the pieces to the wind. 'There go the treaties', he exclaimed.

Today we realise that this fireworks display on the 8th January 1848 also marked the beginning of the most important phase in the relationship of the peoples in the area of contact. On that day the whites of South Africa took upon themselves the responsibility for governing and 'civilising' the blacks. The degree of effectiveness with which they performed this self-appointed task is at the root of all controversy about 'uplift'.

Missionaries took the lead – preaching the Gospel, baptising converts and building thatched churches. They also set up small printing presses and began to give written form to the dialects of the tribes. Round them they saw women tilling the fields with their hoes and brewing beer for their husbands; and young boys who should have been at school, herding the cattle. In an attempt to improve the primitive methods of farming, the Rev. William Shaw, doyen of Wesleyan missionaries, introduced the plough to the Cape Nguni, which had unexpected consequences. It could till more soil faster and better than many women with hoes, so that there was no longer any need for a man to have many wives to work his land. Sir Harry Smith had ordered the chiefs to 'abolish the sin of buying wives' and the missionaries preached with much fervour against it. None of them understood that *lobola* (bridewealth) was in no way a purchase transaction but a symbol that legitimised the union and assured certain rights for both man and wife. But quite possibly it was the plough as much as the orders and exhortations that began to reduce polygamy.

22

Secondly, the use of the plough took on rapidly and arable land spread into the grazing areas. The chiefs realised its value, and by 1855 Sir George Grey had to give the Chief, Sandile, a plough at his request. New crops – including wheat, vegetables and fruit trees – were introduced. The industrious Fingoes were able to hold an agricultural show on the Queen's birthday in 1873 – a demonstration of loyalty and progress of which Her Majesty was most probably unaware. What was then earnestly believed to be the good work of teaching the new agriculture to the tribes continued until 1894, when even more rapid progress was made in terms of the Glen Grey Act, which divided what is now the Transkei into 18 territories. Each was given a demonstrator who had been trained at the small agricultural schools of Tsolo and Teko. He was armed with a plough, harrow and one-row planter and cultivator.

What the ardent reformers from the mild climate of the British Isles did not appreciate was that the plough, in an area of heavy rainfall, could become a poison fang in the soil. The black man believed that up-and-down hill ploughing required less effort than contour-ploughing, with the result that the topsoil began to wash away in the thunderstorms. The furrows became deep dongas ribbing the steep hills. Soil erosion soon made this fertile landscape look like a skeleton of dead earth. The ceremonial ox had become a draught-beast, inspanned to the plough and the wooden sledge that left further scars on the grass cover.

Veterinary science began to control endemic disease and there was no great epizootic, until the rinderpest destroyed the herds in 1897. More than a decade later, when the agriculturists of what was now the Union of South Africa became aware of the threat of soil erosion to the black rural areas, the cures they proposed – especially stock limitation – were resisted all along the Green Belt. The people argued that they had too little land, not too many cattle. Cattle, more cattle, was their highest good and the most ardent desire of every Nguni. The herdsman's shroud must be a hide blanket; and his grave dug in the wet manure of the cattle kraal, with a fat ox slaughtered as viaticum for his spirit on its long journey. He would not rest, like the world's first peasants of the Tigris-Euphrates Valley, in the topsoil's aphar – the dust he came out of and to which he was doomed to return.

Such cattlemen did not take readily to Rothamstead's ideas of scientific farming. But soil conservation was needed to make the land carry more people. From 1930 onwards the Nguni heard that these new ways were what the chiefs in 'the big hut' next to Cape Town's avenue of old oaks wanted. After almost three centuries of destruction of the environment the white rulers of South Africa began to understand that conservation was the cement which would keep the pieces of the human mosaic in place. If the soil of the black homelands was allowed to wash away in a blood-red torrent down to the Indian Ocean, a black tide of starving Nguni would turn away from the strip of coast and ripple inland over the mountains to the cities, where a man could get food and shelter by selling his muscle power to dig in the depths of the mines or build up the concrete skeletons of the skyscrapers.

But contact and adaption along a border is only one chapter in the story of peoples and cultures meeting in South Africa. In Natal, which the Voortrekkers reached with their long, out-flanking movement, events took another path. They were to strike at the territorial heart of these Nguni tribes, the military kraals of the Zulu chiefs. And as the wagons moved down the Drakensberg Mountains, the commandants gave names to the landmarks in the peaceful setting. But during the wars of the next half century these very names would become known to the world as battlefields – the grassed hump of Majuba, the gentle Bloukrans where wagons would flame on the banks and women and children die in a massacre, and the big river, flowing down from the Balelasberg, would be red with the blood of revenge. Then the British threw their redcoats against an enemy who seemed almost invincible and left the tragic memories of Isandhlwana and Rorke's Drift on the maps of history. But it was not only Zulu blood that flowed. At the turn of the century, as Boer fought Briton on this same good green earth, the old names would again flame as battlefields in the news headlines – Elandslaagte, Colenso and Spioenkop.

In fact, Natal is one of the regions of southern Africa where warfare resulted in a drastic decrease of population. It began with the maraudings of the brilliant and despotic Zulu chief, Shaka, often incorrectly interpreted as mere manifestations of savage sadism. To obtain the sanction of more and more Nguni tribes for his wars, Shaka must also have taken advantage of the ecological stresses that were at work – the grazing needs of the enormous herds of cattle and the search for new bush to burn so that the crops of sorghum, millet and maize could feed the people.

And numbers were also the mainspring which determined the policy the white rulers adopted towards the blacks. The American Indian, the Maori and the Australian 'Blackfellow' would always be a small segment of the demographic whole. But in South Africa the obvious biological fact was that the birth-rate of the black man was higher and that he was growing numerically much faster than the whites, who were beginning to own the largest share of the land. An attempt would therefore have to be made to impart Western technology to the blacks in order to increase the carrying capacity of their territory. This in turn necessitated a switch from extensive cattle ranching to more intensive arable farming.

The demographic dilemma evolved fairly rapidly. After the Battle of Blood River in 1838, 6 000 whites established their rule in Natal over about 25 000 blacks. But within seven years the influx from Zululand, north of the Tugela River, had reached an annual total of 80 000. When Sir Theophilus Shepstone, a great administrator, went at great peril to himself to Cetshwayo in 1873, the Zulu nation already numbered about 600 000. But only 17 years before they were so few that a commission appointed to assign lands to them had toyed with the idea of sending them southwards into Pondoland. This would have been a territorial amalgamation of the coastal Nguni. But to meet the growing demand for labour, it was decided instead to establish six locations with a total area of about half a million hectares. The grand mosaic was becoming a rather tattered patchwork – and this is what the present generation of South Africans have inherited from men who had so little knowledge of the territorial imperatives of the black tribes.

The British governors identified and wrote much about the two main problems of the 'patchwork' locations: that the tribal system of communal ownership of land, with the chiefs indicating each man's share, could not be continued; and that there would have to be more intensive production. The 1847 Commission accordingly recommended individual tenure 'to make it necessary for the Bantu to earn money by work on the farms to buy a holding'. The warrior-herdsmen, who had roamed far away from the forests into the grasslands, were to lay aside their shields and stabbing assegais, to become peasants doing women's work with a hoe. Once again the transformation scene of this geopolitical pantomime would be performed with the aid of the magic wand of education. The harlequins, changing from *umuTsha* (loin coverings of skin or fibre) to cast-off trousers, would be taught their new rôle by 'the establishment of industrial schools in each village to instruct them in the elements of gardening and agriculture as well as some of the more useful and easy trades'. But nobody waved the wand.

However, a foreign cousin of the black's own grain sorghum, the tall *Saccharum* genus of the *Andropogoneae* grass tribe, would come to wave its silky inflorescence over the Natal hills as a substitute for the magic wand. Instead of more education there was to be more work. An Englishman, Edmund Morewood, first grew sugar-cane in Natal, but the yields were low and a form of smut threatened the crop. Then the patient trial-and-error experiments of Daniel de Pass, the first notable Jewish farmer in South Africa, resulted in the discovery in 1883 that the Uba strain from India could save the industry from the threat of disease.

Since then the canefields have spread over the hills as the planters felled the trees of the coastal forest – the patriarchal umdoni, the shady albizia, the fearsome strangler fig, the red milkwood, the monkey orange and the ironwood, more than 200 species of the richest tree flora in South Africa. But these canefields, from the planting of the sets to the reaping of the crop with pangas, required a great deal of manual labour; and the Zulu, unlike the Pondo from the south, could not be persuaded that back-breaking labour in the hot sun was the ultimate destiny and salvation of the Nguni herdsman.

As a result, a new dimension was added to the labour force of Natal and the complexity of its racial and religious pattern. In 1860 the planters secured legal permission to bring indentured coolie labour from India.

They came by the boatload into Port Natal. Tamil-speaking Indians from the Madras Coast, professing Hinduism, were most numerous; but there were also many Hindu speakers from North India and Telegus from the south. Shortly afterwards others came out at their own expense, 'passenger' Indians that included many Muslim Gujaratis from Bombay. Today these shrewd traders form a wealthy class which constitutes nearly a fifth of the Indian population. The conditions under which they came allowed them to choose their own job after five years in the canefields; after ten years they were entitled to a free return passage. In 1927 an attempt was made to induce them to return by the offer of a bonus in addition to the free passage. During the following 20 years several thousand took advantage of the scheme. But the others were already South Africans, conscious of the good things as well as the evils of the land, and they remained to form yet another piece in the human mosaic.

The plan to make the Indians go back was primarily an attempt to simplify the political and sociological aspects of the pattern. But pressure on the land was also beginning to be felt. On maps that use dots to indicate population density, the Green Coast had become a shadowy area and in Natal the dots had merged into solid masses. When the National Party Government came to power in 1948, their planners looked at the figures of five census returns taken from 1904 to 1946. During these 42 years the annual rate of increase of the whites had been 2,6 per cent, and that of the other peoples 2,9 per cent. For the whole country, the number of people per square kilometre had risen from 7 to 18. The Indians, 620 000 of them in 1970, were about 3 per cent of the total population and the largest settlement of Indians outside of India anywhere in the world.

From the Transkei to Swaziland the immediate safeguard appeared to be to devise an agricultural system which would produce more food, and absorb more labour without ruining the soil. The canefields spread out, but they had one great disadvantage: here was a food crop, sugar, which could not become a staple diet, like rice and wheat and maize, to nourish a large number of people. So Natal is now dreaming new dreams and drawing more blueprints in an attempt to evolve regional plans, using its great wealth of water to attract industries, to draw the herdsman and the ploughman to the production line.

4

The mountain kingdom

Dingane, the Zulu King, set his dancing warriors on Piet Retief, the Voortrekker leader, and his men with the command: '*Babulaleni abathakathi!*' (Kill the wizards!); and for generations those words have conjured up an image of disembowelled white men being dragged up KwaMatiwane Hill, the place of execution. In South African history, the ten syllables of the Zulu tongue became the notes of a *danse macabre,* performed with burning wagons for a background. They created a highlight of sound in the conception of the Zulus as a tribe of barbarous, treacherous savages. But in contrast with that unforgotten command, there are three other words, the motto of the Sotho: *Khotso, Pula, Nala* – a prayer for peace, rain and good harvests. Such a comparison between the Zulu as a predator nation and the Sotho as peaceful builders is, however, not entirely justified.

It is the creation mainly of the Rev. E. Casalis, a French missionary, who spent 23 years among the Sotho and published a book about them in 1861. The historian Theal conceded that 'there is no better book in existence concerning the habits and the customs of the Basuto people'. But he, too, doubted the validity of the political conclusions. The Frenchman's portrait of Moshweshwe, the Sotho Chief, who ruled from Thaba Bosiu (The Hill at Night), is of a man 'having a noble and dignified deportment; his features bespoke habits of reflection and command, and a benevolent smile played upon his lips.' But Moshweshwe had attained that position as a result of his skill in the chase and the assistance of a band of hunters, which became an efficient war machine during the years when the Highveld was red with blood.

For Moshweshwe it was the throwing assegai, not his lineage, that made him chief; and in the beginning he must have used it with as much skill as his subsequent diplomacy. As the supreme example of this diplomacy and sagacity, Casalis describes an attack made by Mzilikazi's *impis* (regiments) on the pentagon-shaped Basotho mountain stronghold. Twice the Matabele were repulsed by an avalanche of basalt boulders, and when they retreated, Moshweshwe sent them a gift of fat oxen with the message: 'Moshweshwe salutes you. Supposing that hunger has brought you into this country, he sends you these cattle, that you may eat them on your way home.' The Matabele remembered the man who had rolled down rocks on their heads and then sent them food. They never attacked him again.

The significance of the message lay not so much in its display of diplomacy as in Moshweshwe's realisation that hunger was the major cause of war among the Sotho – the black tribes to the west of the great escarpment, the children of southern Africa's prairies, where herds of game were to be found in far greater abundance than bison on the American plains. This high eastern border is the roof of South Africa – a summit plateau at 1 200 m to 3 282 m above sea level, dissected by the headwaters of the Orange River. In summer this tundra is boggy, but it freezes hard under periodic winter snowfalls, and snow glitters on the castellated lava and sandstone krantzes. When migrating blacks had looked up at the white rim of the plateau from their fires in the thorn bush to the east they would have known that this cold country was not a good place to go to. A thousand metres lower, to the north and west of the Maluti Mountains, near the headwaters of the Caledon and Wilge Rivers, there was warmer country and better soil, the beginning of the grassland plains.

Lists of the names of the tribes that murdered the Bushmen and hunted the game of the dusty, wind-blown region have been compiled. Yet today little more than names remain of these groups of people that destroyed one another at the beginning of the 19th century as wars flared and raiding *impis* swept up and down from the Orange to the Vaal River. It is impossible to tell how many people died by the club and the assegai. The numbers of the Tlokwa, one of the mountain tribes, are estimated to have been reduced from 130 000 to less than 15 000. A conservative estimate is that 300 000 were killed in the mountains of what is now Lesotho and in the north-east of the present Orange Free State. In Shaka's country, the green belt between the mountains and the sea, at least half a million perished. One of Theal's maps, compiled in 1890, is laconically titled '*Country nearly depopulated by the Zulu wars before 1834*'. Not inappropriately, the dotted outline resembles a mighty fist. The wrist is formed by the Tugela and Umzimvubu Rivers and the knuckles bend with the sweep of the Limpopo, down along the mountains and back to the Tugela.

An attempt might possibly be made to explain the deep-rooted causes of these three decades of killing in terms of the impulses of territorial aggression. The tribes were almost identical in culture, language, law and religion, but they formed groups that sought greater identity and security. Boundaries were only vaguely defined, like those of the widow birds of the Themeda grassland, which may be why the Sotho have a proverb: 'All countries are borders.' War has always been an expression of the territorial imperative – in southern Africa a hurling of assegais at long distances with appropriate gestures of defiance. Then Shaka perfected the strategy of the stabbing assegai and taught the warriors to get in close and kill – for such permanent regiments war became an escape from boredom. On the other hand, the environmentalist may have a different explanation. The climate of this country is such that large regions are afflicted by unpredictable periodic droughts when the veld cannot carry the herds and the crops die in the hot topsoil. Then it became necessary to raid the food supplies of more fortunate neighbours with territory blessed by good rains. Not a motiveless urge, but the thought of the grain basket and the fat ox may well have sent the *impis* on the warpath.

Whatever the cause of the flare-up of killing may have been, its geopolitical consequences are obvious: they brought Moshweshwe to power on his mountain stronghold and they created a population vacuum – a large area of scorched earth into which the Voortrekkers could move and ultimately come to settle. For Moshweshwe the mountain with its steep basalt krantzes was as much a weapon as a fortress. It was, like the stabbing assegai, a new invention in African warfare – a weapon of defence, not offence. It could resist the best *impis,* whose own food supplies on the march were insufficient for a long siege. It was a safe place for Moshweshwe to assemble his *khotla* (court) and his counsellors to make and apply laws and expound the philosophy that the hard life of a hunter-warrior had taught him. Certainly, there was much wisdom – and also cunning, caution and forethought. He was able to offer emissaries from the shattered tribes not only security but the greater identity of budding nationhood. Among the Sotho the affairs of state were much more democratic than those of the military dictatorships of the Nguni, although they, too, had a system of counsellors to limit the excesses of chiefly office.

Moshweshwe welcomed all who submitted to him – even those who had become cannibals and taken to the caves during the wars and the famine. His warriors went down the Drakensberg and looted a considerable wealth of cattle from the Tembu clans. His brother struck south at a tribe on the banks of the Orange River and carried off all they possessed, including their women and children. There was much strife and looting before Moshweshwe decided that what his growing nation needed most of all was missionaries, the 'medicine men of the Europeans'. He even attempted to purchase one of these valuable experts by sending a hundred head of cattle to Adam Kok, the Griqua Chief at the little mission town of Philippolis. And when the first pious Frenchmen arrived at Thaba Bosiu in 1831 the white men would not only teach them 'how to make paper speak', but also how to make better use of their natural environment.

In the course of time the Sotho learned to grow wheat by carefully selecting rust-resistant strains out of the fields sown with seed from the South of France. The horse also entered their lives on a considerable scale. These animals, too, adapted themselves to the climate and pastures of the country and evolved the famous Basotho ponies, which even attained some martial glory when British cavalry rode them in the Charge of the Light Brigade. But the Sotho, unlike the Griqua, did not use them to imitate the raiding Boer commando. For them the ponies became pack animals to carry heavy burdens up into the mountains and so added a third dimension to their country. As the population grew, the cold, boggy tundras near the edge of the escarpment became accessible to the shepherds – and to the onslaught of soil erosion.

So rapid was the process of acculturation that the missionaries had good reason to believe that they had opened the road to the first African Utopia. But there was the sound of gunfire to the west. It was obvious to Moshweshwe that this was not the boom of the hunter's elephant gun or of *trekboere* on the move, shooting for the pot. The people of Thaba Nchu mission station, who had watched the long train of wagons turn seaward to Natal, reported that white men with large flocks and herds were coming back to stay. Moshweshwe would soon realise the truth of the saying that all countries are borders.

On missionary advice, the Sotho had virtually become British subjects. Indeed, the treaty Moshweshwe signed in his stronghold on the 13th December 1843 was little more than a useful British pretext for the annexation of the country at the expense of the Orange Free State. But 11 years later the sovereignty was virtually abandoned by Great Britain. Henceforth the borders would be determined by a series of wars and treaties that lasted until 1880. The future of Moshweshwe and his people would be decided by Voortrekker policy; and in essence this consisted of marking off areas – good land, thinly populated – for predominantly white occupation, while retaining a sufficient force of farm workers.

In spite of skilful military tactics based on the flat-topped mountain fortresses with their steep krantzes, Moshweshwe lost the war. What is more important, he lost the ecological battle as well. In future the Sotho would no longer plough the valleys of the Caledon River and its tributaries to the west. The area would become known as the Conquered Territory of the Orange Free State – a valuable granary leading a precarious existence on sandy, easily erodible soils. From that time on the growing Sotho population has had to bounce back, uphill into the mountains, where the torrential rains ravage the topsoil turned by the plough on the steep slopes.

5

Scorched earth

In the sweltering Magaliesberg summer of 1829, Mzilikazi emerged from his pandemonium to greet Robert Moffat, the missionary. Eight hundred of his Matabele warriors, beating their shields with the shafts of assegais while they danced like demons in the cattle kraal, suddenly sat down in a profound, disciplined silence. The tyrant, unaware that he was taking the first steps on a straight and narrow path, held the Christian by the arm as they set out towards the approaching wagons. He wanted to find out how they 'walk', for he had never seen a wagon before.

Then the rebel chief, who had sown death across the scorched earth of the Transvaal and Orange Free State, felt the touch of fear. Maybe instinct told him that these white-tented houses, that shook and swayed like elephant bulls, would shape a new destiny for himself and his people. As the wagons drew near, he gave a start and jumped back. Moffat watched the chief closely and saw him staring at the motion, particularly the turning wheels. Once the oxen were unyoked, he held his hand to his mouth in a gesture of amazement and walked up to examine the spokes, the axles, the hubs and the iron rims. The wonder of the wheel, first recorded in Sumerian pictographs of 3 000 B.C., had come to the very hills where a steelworks would be built a century later.

But in 1829 it was a brave act for a Matabele to touch a wheel; and the warriors rose up with an immense burst of applause. They did not expect that within seven years there would be many wagons on the way to test their courage in battle against this strange thing. At first the wagons of the missionaries cut across the veld spoors that became rugged, rutted roads between the far away ocean and Philippolis, Klaarwater and Kuruman. But wherever a missionary builds a church, traders are sure to follow. As Livingstone explained, 'they are mutually dependent, and each aids the work of the other'. These comings and goings included the first scientific expedi-tion, the trek of Dr Andrew Smith, who collected birds and mammals and snakes, and left a strangely dispassionate account of Mzilikazi's execution methods. By the time the hunter-artist Captain Cornwallis Harris arrived, Mzilikazi had withdrawn to the furthest boundary of his territory on the edge of the great thirstland into which he had driven the Sotho tribes. He needed to put distance between himself and Shaka's *impis* raiding from the east, partly to settle an old quarrel but mainly to loot cattle. And from the south the wagons of the Great Trek were advanc-ing in slow stages across the depopulated Highveld *vlaktes*.

There are only fragments of written records to indicate the extent to which Mzilikazi had killed off the tribes that inhabited this region before he continued his trek northwards. He could have enslaved these people, leaving them behind to cultivate their land. But this would have created food supplies for inva-ders. So he used the stabbing assegai of the Zulu instead of the slave chain of the Arab.

When Moffat first journeyed to the capital of the Matabele, he trekked for part of the way along the beautiful slopes of the Magaliesberg – a wedge-shaped mountain chain between the great inland plateau and the Bushveld. He was writing for people who knew John Bunyan's *Pilgrim's Progress* almost as well as they knew the Bible, and his account of the devastation that he beheld reads like a ghastly allegory. There are the Delectable Mountains, the City of Destruction and the Valley of the Shadow of Death in an African setting. The young Scottish missionary is Pilgrim. He treks into a country where there are all the signs that many happy people lived here. But death has come to the valley: 'Now since the invasion of the Mantatis and the terror of the Matabele, it had become the habitation of wild beasts and venomous reptiles, where lions roam at large as if conscious that there are none to oppose, which from the late extirpating wars have become so inured to gorge on human flesh that they are now the terror of the traveller, who hears with dismay his nightly roarings echoed back from the surrounding hills and glens.' Moffat's descrip-tion, however, is not only of mounds of skulls, but also of ruined villages that seem to indicate traces of a culture more advanced than that of the killers. This had been a people rich in cattle and grain who had traded far into the interior.

But Mzilikazi refused to allow the Voortrekker wagons into this population vacuum – a great horseshoe region punched into the heartland of southern Africa by the might of the Nguni fist. He attacked – and then learned that his first fear of the wagon had presaged doom. At Vegkop, one of the heroic moments in Afrikaner history, the Voortrekkers formed a square *laager* (encampment), piled thorn branches between the wheels, and defeated the Matabele army. To recover the cattle they lost, the trekkers also sent out two commandos against Mzilikazi, who was no match for the white man's trinity of power – the wagon,

The Highveld.

the gun and the horse. In utter despair he fled once again, to the north this time, with his Matabele, who had numbered 900 when he set out from Zululand and were now about 80 000. They left more good land for still fewer people.

The immediate sequel was another exodus – the eastward movement of the Great Trek, down the Drakensberg, to occupy that other population vacuum which Dingane and his Zulu had created between the Tugela and Umzimkulu Rivers and which the Trekkers thought of calling 'New Holland'. But Piet Retief and his people were not only following a political bluebird, the dream of a new state with a harbour that opened windows on the world: there were ecological reasons as well. When Dingane asked him why they had left the Highveld where there were no people, the Voortrekker leader replied that in the cold winters the rivers dried up so that they had no water; nor was there any firewood to warm the houses.

And when, after the tragedies of Natal, the Voortrekkers began to trickle back to the plateau country, those three ecological factors would play an important part in their choice of a place to build a farmhouse and settle for good. This population distribution was largely determined by the fact that the whites were bread-eaters. They did not relish the black man's sorghum, a plant that was for centuries adapted to African conditions and closed up its ears to resist the drought. Their need was for running water to irrigate a small field of wheat – enough to produce stone-ground meal loaves baked in the outdoor clay ovens. At the *saailaer* (sowing *laager*) on the banks of the Little

Tugela in Natal, Gert Maritz built a small dam and sowed wheat, although the Zulu *impis* were massing to attack. Potgieter, when he led the commando against Mzilikazi, had seen one of the wonders of the Western Transvaal, and he went back to that place, the *Mooirivier* – the beautiful river. It is fed by a crystal-clear stream that gushes all the year round from beneath a dolomite ledge, which must have reminded these pious farmers of the rock that Moses struck to bring water to the desert. On the banks of the Mooi River they laid out a town – the present-day Potchefstroom – and planted wheat. Along the Suikerbosrand and the Witwatersrand smaller streams flowed out of the quartzites into the *vleis* (swampy lowlands); and these, too, were the sites for the Highveld's new farms.

To keep out the buck that came to graze the young wheat at night, they surrounded the fields with stone walls. Much of this building material was taken from old hilltop 'kraals' – structures erected more than six centuries before by an Iron Age civilisation which had vanished in the turmoil of the veld and its wars. The pattern of the Voortrekker farms can still be traced from the remains of the walls. There is the wheat field and next to it the orchard; and the main water-furrow was usually fed from a fountain or from a small dam in a kloof. Beside the furrows they planted acorns brought from the Cape. Today the huge oaks are like symbols of the birthplace of the Afrikaner nation, transplanted to a new and harsher heartland.

It is not yet – and it may never become – a unified geographical territory, but the psychological habitat of that nation now spreads out from Van Riebeeck's garden to outposts that were established by invaders, like the Thirstland Trekkers and the Angola Boers – as far north as the Kunene and Zambezi Rivers. Within its borders the Highvelders of the Transvaal and Orange Free State have become a cultural type, as distinct as the people of the Cape valleys, the Swartland and the Karoo. Climate and soil, diet and the work that had to be done to subdue the environment were like cupped hands guiding the potter's clay on the wheel of civilisation. But most important of all in the moulding of the Highvelders were the traditions and legends, as told by fathers to their sons, of the *worstelstryd van die wordingsjare* – the struggle of the years of becoming. And in many ways it was a Titanic battle compared with the adaptation of men and vineyards to the land of the Hottentots and Bushmen.

The Transvaal was a region without the borders to make it a country in the geopolitical sense when the Voortrekkers came back. To the west of Potchefstroom, the first Highveld town, there was in 1840 only the vaguely defined barrier of 'the Thirstland'; to the east expansion was halted in 1844 by an agreement that they would not come closer than four days' journey from any Portuguese harbour; down the Drakensberg the British were infiltrating Natal; and to the south there was the menace of Moshweshwe on his mountain and beyond the Orange River there slumbered the Cape, which they had left to escape from the rule and ideas of the new conquerors.

It was a population vacuum without walls; and, together with the Voortrekkers, the tribes that had fled from Mzilikazi began filtering back from the Kalahari which had been a refuge for many people. Early travellers, such as J. Stuart, who visited the Transvaal in 1854, estimated that there were not more than 100 000 people in the country. By 1868, F. Jeppe and A. A. Anderson had pushed the total up to about 300 000; and then the more reliable estimate that was made before the war of 1881 placed the total number of blacks at 750 000. Since the area of the young Republic, between the Vaal and the Orange Rivers, was only a little smaller than present-day Italy, a wagon could travel for weeks from the kraal of one black chief to the next, most of whose people had taken shelter in the Bushveld. There were only a few spoors of Baralong herdsmen and Bushmen hunters in the frost of the Highveld's winters.

The cold, the lack of water points and the hard soil, which their wooden ploughs could not turn, still kept the first white Highvelders along the fringe of watered hills to the north. They led a kind of double life; and it was a hard one. Once the wheat had been reaped with sickles, threshed with flails and ground between round stones, the preparations for the autumn trek down the escarpment to the Bushveld began. The women baked *beskuit* (dried biscuits) and canned the yellow peaches, while the men checked their guns and wagons. Before the arrival of iron axles in 1848 the wagons still had wooden ones and could carry a load of only about 1 000 kg. But they sagged when the trek began and would be still more heavily laden with ivory, skins and biltong on the return journey. This movement was not true nomadism: it was more of a seasonal migration away from the grass of the sour Bankeveld, which could not keep their herds in condition through the winter. Even when they moved south, into the sweet veld, the Bushveld winter had become such a deep-rooted custom that May was still the month when the wagons were inspanned to seek a change of climate and scene.

This trek was one of the reasons why the Highveld farming system remained unstable for many years. During the cold months, when the veld was brown, there was no smoke from the chimneys of the *hartbeeshuise* and the cattle and sheep kraals were empty. The *hartbeeshuis*, with its mud walls and thatched roof, had been with them since the days when their fathers were *trekboere* and then *grensboere*. It was a symbol of impermanence. The men who built it were always afraid that they might suddenly have to move on again to spend months with their wagons forming part of the *laager* wall. Although the fear was often unfounded, they did not trust Moshweshwe and the other chiefs returning to the land.

In these circumstances, poverty was widespread and progress was slow at first. But the attempts they had made to organise this scattered Trekker society had given it a base of order and law, even if prosperity was slow in coming. Soon after their return from Natal, small republics, which they called *maatskappye*, were established at Ohrigstad, Soutpansberg, Magaliesberg and Potchefstroom, the only cold-country centre. Of the original 300 heads of families to leave Natal more than 200 came to Potchefstroom, named after their famous leader Hendrik Potgieter, a powerful man, who had a way with him. The first farms along the Mooi River were allocated in 1838 and within 16 years the white population of the town numbered over 2 000. But the stands were like small farms whose owners grew wheat under irrigation, tobacco, quinces, apricots, figs and grapes. The town had a market and became a centre of trade – especially in ivory and hides.

And the hunters who came to sell their trophies in Potchefstroom were changing the whole ecology of the Highveld. When the white man first moved in it was still the grassland habitat of vast free-roaming herds of game, probably the greatest biomass of mammals that the world has ever known. Dr Andrew Smith, the explorer, had been impressed by the great numbers of blesbok and the myriads of springbok that flickered like fragments of sunlight when they pranced and wheeled over the veld. Captain Cornwallis Harris had admired the herds of stately eland 'that walked like domestic cattle' and the black wildebeest that galloped across the landscape like troops of cavalry. The Voortrekkers themselves had named the *Vetrivier* after the fat game that glistened on its banks. But this luxuriance of wildlife was becoming wagon loads of horns, skins, tusks, karosses, thongs and ostrich feathers for the market at Potchefstroom.

The money they earned from the game they shot was the main income of the Transvaal's farmers, and every farmer was also a hunter – on the Highveld in summer and in the Bushveld in winter. It was good money. The white feathers of a cock ostrich were worth about R20 and those of a hen R4; rhino horns fetched 15 cents a pound; and ivory was R50 a hundredweight. But the supply of 'raw material' for the trade dwindled rapidly, as can be seen from the value of ivory exported through Port Natal: R80 000 in 1862; R52 000 in 1864; R38 000 in 1865; R13 000 in 1866; and R11 000 in 1867. To supply the value of ivory for this last export year, about 350 elephant must have been shot. Only the herds of antelope seemed almost inexhaustible and as late as 1872 the hides of 250 000 buck were sent from the Highveld to the port.

Today this ruthless hunting can be interpreted as the overexploitation of a renewable natural resource. The hunters themselves were ignorant of the laws of Nature's balance. But even if they had known how to conserve the herds by merely culling the increase, it is more than doubtful whether they would have done so, for the grasslands could be used in more practical ways. Just as the Americans felled the forests to plant corn, so the Boers cleared out the game to bring in sheep. By 1880 J. A. Froude would write: 'Their wealth is sheep and cattle.'

But the life of the Transvaal's hunter-farmers had another side-effect: it made them deadly accurate sharpshooters for military purposes, as they showed at Majuba, and again when the Anglo-Boer War (1899-1902), which has euphemistically been called 'the last gentleman's war', was fought on the open veld.

This later war left more than blood and the spoors of gun-carriage wheels on the grasslands of the Highveld. Farmhouses were burned systematically, and livestock slaughtered to supply the Tommies with meat and deprive the commandos of biltong, one of the main items in their scanty commissariat. After the Peace of Vereeniging, the farmers returned to a good earth that had been scorched once again. They had to reconstruct the agricultural system which had evolved from the days when Potgieter's people had settled on the banks of the Mooi River and were beginning to prosper.

That the Transvaal Boers were unable to create a viable state before the discovery of the gold of the Witwatersrand is incorrect. The population statistics alone disprove it. In 1873 there were about 30 000 whites north of the Vaal River. Thirteen years later, in 1886 when gold mining began, the number had already doubled. People do not immigrate into a country threatened with eternal poverty. The *hartbeeshuis* was disappearing and farmhouses of cut sandstone with corrugated iron roofs, still so typical of the Highveld landscape, were beginning to appear. A new type, *die welgestelde boer,* a man of substance, was emerging from the battle to tame and develop the veld. In 1870 he was described as owning about 500 sheep and 200 head of cattle. But ten years later, in the sheep country of the Eastern Transvaal, the Rev. Cachet found some of the *welgestelde* men shearing flocks of 3 000. German settlers at Lüneburg were importing pedigree rams and by 1881 the Transvaal's yearly production of wool had reached 25 000 bales. It stimulated the demand for a railway line to Lourenço Marques (Maputo), for a spirited, productive people cannot be cut off from the sea. But up to now transport requirements had been met by the *transportryer,* the transport driver with his wagons – another romantic Highveld figure.

Postal communications between the developing *dorpe,* the small towns, were maintained by the *poskar* (post cart), which sounded a bugle when it approached; and it is as much a part of the folk memories of the Highvelders as the fish carts of Cape Town and the seaweed 'bugle' that the Malay fishermen used. But naturally, the trumpet which heralded the coming of news

was made of copper in the progressive Transvaal! The Republic had already begun to use stamps on the 1st January 1870, and four years later there were 37 towns with post offices. Letters drew widespread families closer together, from Pilgrim's Rest in the north to Bloemhof on the Vaal River; they speeded up personal business and stimulated commerce; and, most important of all, the post brought the *Staatscourant,* the official organ which indicated what the *Volksraad* (House of Assembly) was planning for the country.

The service was slow at first and a post cart took 31 hours from Potchefstroom to Pretoria, the new capital which the Volksraad had ordered to be laid out in 1855. But it brought a unity to the country second only in effect to the creation of a capital. When Andries François du Toit began to survey the wide streets in which an ox wagon could turn, it was also a symbolical act that indicated that the Great Trek had ended. The little republics had come together at last and Pretoria, like Bloemfontein, was the heart of a new heartland.

Of course, it would be wrong to contend that without the wealth of the gold mines the pioneer subsistence farms would have advanced as rapidly as they did to modern agricultural units. There were too few people to provide a market. In 1870, between the Cape and the Limpopo River, 317 000 whites produced their food on their own land. The beginning of small-scale gold mining in the Transvaal Bushveld in 1873, the finding in the Cape of the first diamond in 1867 and then the discovery of the seemingly inexhaustible gold reefs of the Witwatersrand in 1886, brought not only an inflow of population but also commercially viable railways south and east. Johannesburg, with its growth pains, developed hunger pangs, which the farmers could only satisfy by 'mining' the topsoil in turn.

In the Transvaal this agricultural-mining phase of development lasted from 1873 to 1914, when new factories added to the demand for agricultural products. The plough and the barbed wire fence, like a ferocious fang and claw, began to change the Highveld landscape more radically than the hunters with their guns. In less than 80 years the grasslands were transformed, and the king of man-made grasses, the maize plant, probed the blue skies with its male spikelets over an area almost twice the size of Holland. In 1947 the gold mines were spending R14 million on produce of the soil. Nature's grasses, the veld gold on which the Voortrekkers had grazed their flocks and herds, were assets which only the conservationists dreamed of using to restore fertility and produce even greater wealth.

The Atomic and Space Age Highveld has changed and grown so much that it is the wealthiest region in Africa. In the south, near the drifts through which Voortrekker wagons forded the Orange River, have arisen the concrete dams of a great power-irrigation project; in the centre, on the north and south banks of the Vaal River, there is a cluster of cities and towns that may well become a metropolitan complex as large as present-day New York or Tokyo; and in the east, tapping the water of distant rivers, there are the coal-burning power stations, which feed a network that covers almost the whole country. The population vacuum that Mzilikazi made has drawn into it not only the Voortrekkers and the tribes that fled from his tyranny, but immigrants from all over the world. In the midst of this diversity, where the pieces of the human mosaic overlap, it is difficult to trace the original pattern or define the true Highvelders – the people who pioneered and ruled this region for so long.

But it is possible, almost like an archaeologist digging the first trench of his grid, to bring them to light. They generally do not live in towns, but they are always close to the seats of power, supplying the country with prime ministers and state presidents. They are surrounded by the winds of change, but memories and traditions remain their lodestone. They adapt, but with all the caution of a herd of springbok entering a new territory to drink at a strange water-hole.

It is revealing to dig such a trench between Bethal and Middelburg, a line that runs closely parallel to the route the Trichardts followed when they headed the Great Trek into the unknown, down the divide between the Vaal and Olifants Rivers and into the Bushveld. Here Karel, the leader's eldest son, saw one of the jewels of the Highveld landscape – a fountain that gushed from under a sandstone ledge to feed a broad *vlei*, where gold and scarlet bishop birds flashed among the reeds and bulrushes. And later, after he had wandered up and down Africa, he came back to that place and named it Koringfontein – the wheat fountain. He died there, and his grave in Middelburg is still almost a shrine. But his memory lingers with the veld life that remains – the call of the kiewiet in the night or of the clapper lark rising up into the mists. His sons and grandsons lived there and they, too, led the water from the fountain to the wheatfields and listened to the veld talking. But for his great-grandchildren these sounds were muted by the soft hum of steam turbines, for Koringfontein has become a great power-station and its smoke and steam drift over the *vlei*.

Close by there is the farm Blesbokvlakte, which the Goosens named after the great herd of these buck that grazed there until 1910 when the barbed wire fences came. They were Voortrekkers, too, and had been with Gert Maritz when he sowed the field of wheat outside the *saailaer* on the banks of the distant Little Tugela in Natal. But they became poor when rinderpest killed their livestock in 1895 and they trekked to the towns. As a memory of their occupation they left behind a dam, which still holds water, a quince hedge and a few gnarled old apricot trees. It was the beginning of the Afrikaner's drift to the towns that swelled to a flood in the great depression of 1929-1932.

The Anglo-Boer War also raged there and burned deep scars in the hearts of the people. For years the door stoppers in the sandstone farmhouse on Blesbokvlakte were shrapnel shells which the children had picked up on the battlefield of Blinkpan near the cemetery where the British had buried their dead. And to that farmhouse also came Landdrost Gert du Toit to tell his grandchildren how their mother, Natie, had been in the *laager* that was formed to protect the women when the burghers went into the Bushveld to fight Sekhukhune in one of the last Kaffir Wars. He reminisced about Majuba, and showed the button he had cut from General Sir George Pomeroy Colley's coat when he stood guard beside the body. Then his son Dawid would show the young generation the rifle he had taken from a Jameson raider when they surrendered. The flames that flickered in the hearth during the cold winter evenings when the old people talked seemed to come alive with battle images of the Great Trek and the Anglo-Boer War, which had produced a new type of political leader in South Africa – the generals and commandants who were its heroes. Commandant Jack Hindon, destroyer of so many British armoured trains, had once sheltered in that farmhouse; and both General Botha and General Hertzog had used its wide stoep for a political meeting. But now a new fire burns in the hearth at Blesbokvlakte. It is fed from Blesbok Colliery, which sends trainloads of coking coal to the ovens of the steelworks at Pretoria and Vanderbijlpark. In the midst of such change, it is not the memories of wars that are an anchor, but the thoughts of victories won.

Since even greater changes lie ahead for the Highvelders, who still wield great power in South Africa, it is important to know how they will react. In their lives there were seasonal changes, too – calamities that came and went and are not to be confused with the trend of the Big Plan, the destiny in which all of them believe. They had seen the green of spring, when the September lambs frolicked on the veld, followed by the dust storms of drought; they had seen the maize, shedding pollen, covered by a white sheet of hail from the thunderclouds; they had seen plenty followed by poverty and starvation, but out of it all the Highveld had emerged stronger than ever. They have been children of the living veld ever since the first wagons left their spoors; and although they have changed the outlines of the landscape, the rhythm of the veld is in their blood and in their hearts.

It is difficult to conceive that such a people will take readily to the rhythm of the production line or the wheels of industry while they have a field to plough and veld to graze.

6

The Bushveld

Glossina morsitans, the deadly tsetse fly, came into the lives of the Voortrekkers on Thursday the 2nd November 1837. The leader of that advance trek, old Louis Trichardt, with the awe that men feel when they encounter a new, nameless enemy, has recorded the event in detail in his diary. His young son, Petrus, showed him an insect, which flew away when he opened his hand. But the hawk-eyed Bushman herdsman had also seen it near the wagons. They debated whether it was 'the fly that kills cattle' against which the Knobnose tribe had warned them. Within four months their oxen showed symptoms of black diarrhoea; and then they knew that the trek across the Lowveld would be a race against the sickness of the cattle if the wagons were to reach Delagoa Bay, the harbour they were looking for. But they were themselves fated to die in those swamps – victims of other insects lethal to man, *Anopheles gambiae* and *A. funestus,* the malaria mosquitoes.

The tsetse fly, probably more than the mosquito, presented a barrier to the northward migration of the white South Africans of the 19th century. Men may die and be buried beside the trail while the trek moves on, but if the oxen die the wagons come to a standstill. And the Voortrekkers, unlike the explorers of Central Africa, never used native porters as beasts of burden. The diary of Trichardt, written without any thought of the propaganda battles of the present age, shows how patriarchal their attitude was towards their Bushman and black servants. Of course, in the case of Trichardt, he turned east to find a harbour. But others wanted to keep on moving north, almost as if the *trekgees,* a kind of migratory instinct, was driving them forward. One group, who kept on while the swallows passed overhead, turned this northward urge into a religious pilgrimage. They called themselves the *Jerusalemgangers,* and their ultimate objective was the Holy City. But their graves are beside wagon spoors that faded in the fly country.

Even Hendrik Potgieter stayed for no more than three years

near that lovely river and the town named after him. He moved to the Magaliesberg, where the town of Rustenburg was founded in 1850 – fertile, well-watered land on which citrus and tobacco were planted and prospered. But even that vale, named by men who had found peace, was not lush enough for him. The old lion of the trek, driven by dreams of greatness, went further afield to a territory where the hunting was better still. They would soon hear his roar in the Soutpansberg, where he had visited the Trichardts when he made an incredible reconnaissance on horseback, almost as far as the Zimbabwe ruins – a ride of about 3 200 kilometres – in 100 days.

Potgieter himself was too practical a man to think of all this moving about as the manifestation of an inner *trekgees.* He had seen good country – and he had an eye for the beauty and promise of nature – when he visited his friend, Trichardt. He had heard of the thriving ivory trade, and he, too, wanted a harbour for the country. So he headed for Ohrigstad, a village that had been laid out in the heart of the Bushveld in 1845 on land bought from Sekwati, the Pedi chief, land which was part of the population vacuum. Sekwati, attacked by Mzilikazi, had fled beyond the Limpopo River, returned when the Matabele might was broken, and then, like Moshweshwe, gathered the scattered tribes together to form the Pedi nation. And Sekwati could not have been too pleased with the land deal. In 1846 Potgieter attacked him and looted 8 000 cattle and 6 000 goats.

In Ohrigstad the people, who had increased to about 300 in a year, dug a trench to defend the one long street of the village from attack. But the malaria mosquitoes lurking in the bush could not be fought with guns. Every year people got 'the fever' – or 'Delagoa Bay fever', as they called the sickness – which flared up into the epidemic of 1849. By 1850 Ohrigstad was deserted and there were 42 graves in the cemetery.

Half a degree north of the Tropic of Capricorn, in an open plain on the slopes of the Soutpansberg, they then built Schoemansdal, which soon began to thrive. It became the 'ivory capital' of southern Africa. The elephant hunters that set out from there in winter went as far north as legendary Lake Ngami and the banks of the Zambesi River. In 1856 they brought back the tusks of about 1 000 elephants. But although they could destroy the biggest land mammal, they were themselves still harassed and hampered by the tsetse fly. There were large fly belts where they could only hunt on foot and the fly barred the wagon road to Delagoa Bay for the export of ivory.

This frontier village, the Afrikaner *dorp* which was then furthest north in Africa, drew adventurers and also distinguished visitors, like Joaquim de Santa Rita Montanha, a Portuguese emissary. They found anything but a *dorp* atmosphere. Montanha estimated that in 1855 there were about 1 800 people in the district, 'of whom 300 can bear arms' – a handy little police reserve in that kind of country. Every May the farmers went to town for the fair. Then there would arrive the *smouse* – the door-to-door hucksters of veld and bush – who often had to shoot lions in order to peddle their goods in safety from farm to farm and dorp to dorp. They brought dress materials for the women – mostly black, because they mourned for distant relations – and ribbed corduroy for the men. But a better impression of the business side of Schoemansdal is given by Montanha's estimates of yearly purchases: 12 500 kilograms of gunpowder, 20 000 kilograms of lead, 5 000 kilograms of sugar and 2 500 kilograms of coffee.

After the winter, the people who had made merry at the fair waited in trepidation for the symptoms of the fever – the waves of rising temperature, the rigor and the splitting headaches. During wet summers, when the onslaught was particularly severe, they left Schoemansdal for higher ground. There they formed a huge laager to ward off not Matabele and Zulu assegais but the deadly sting of a little insect. The Northern Sotho tribes were still a menace that came down from mountain kraals, but the fever was the worst enemy of all. In 1867 Schoemansdal was abandoned and Chief Katlakter's warriors came and burned the houses and reduced the town to ruins. President Pretorius regarded it as the greatest disaster the republic had sustained.

These people had been on a territorial fringe – the northern curve of the great horseshoe of deserted land – and the blacks were moving in. Their threat took the form of raids and stock-theft, attacks on lonely farms and open warfare. But there was also peaceful penetration. In 1876 *De Volkstem* reported that to the west, in Malitziland, they had moved in between the white farms, settled and begun to hoe the soil to plant sorghum. These Northern Sotho were not numerous, probably less than 100 000 in all, but they were enough to cause serious trouble for the first white settlers. Today the blacks of the northern areas, five large blocks of country and many smaller ones, number almost 1 500 000. They have prospered and multiplied – especially since modern science and DDT beat the malaria mosquitoes. The population density on the 4 000 000 hectares of land they own has risen to an average of 25 per square kilometre, but children play everywhere around the huts and fewer babies are dying. At the end of 1977, they were ready to begin a new phase of change as an independent state.

The Voortrekkers again used the commando, the gun and the *laager* to hold the land. They fought numerous little wars, and many of them died. And although the tribes had been armed by gun-running from the Kimberley Diamond Fields and Delagoa Bay, they were not strong enough to drive the white man back. The Voortrekkers fought the insects, too, mainly by planting bluegum trees, which they believed prevented malaria. But the trees were round the houses and the *Anopheles* lurked along the rivers and in the swamps. The cause of malaria and the use of quinine as an antidote had not yet been discovered. Science was still searching all over the world for a weapon to beat the scourge that had not only hampered the white man's invasion of the tropics, but plagued his first civilisations on the shores of the Mediterranean.

The state of medical knowledge is reflected in a report by Dr James A. Kay, who was sent in 1880 to investigate a malaria epidemic at Nylstroom. He defined malaria as 'a term applied to emanations or invisible effluvia from the surface of the earth, chiefly found in marshy lands, and supposed to be produced by decaying animal or vegetable matter, particularly both'. The mosquito was still king of the Bushveld. It would be at least 50 years before the great eradication campaign that controlled the insect was launched, and man produced an answer to the challenge that this hostile environment presented.

The Bushvelders, applying the lessons they learned from nature, might have been able to beat *Glossina morsitans,* the tsetse fly. This time the gun and deadly accurate shooting – with the plough for an ally – were the weapons in the campaign. They believed simply that destruction of the abundant game in the bush would cause the fly to move away. Like the Highvelders of the open grasslands, they were cleaning up the country – but here the kudu, impala, wildebeest, buffalo, waterbuck, sable and all the other species of antelope were more difficult to get at. This theory was held all over Africa, wherever white men moved into fly country with domestic animals; and millions of head of game, from Zululand through Rhodesia to Kenya, were shot to prove it. The domain of the 20 species of tsetse was huge, covering the greater part of tropical Africa. It ran between a line from the Senegal River to Somaliland in the north and between Angola and Mozambique in the south. But shooting the wild animals on which the flies feed is only one answer to the problem. The other is the destruction of its habitat, the dense, shady bush in which it lives and breeds in profusion.

When the Bushvelders discovered that the fly was killing their cattle they began tilling the fertile soils. Joao Albasini, who came to Ohrigstad in 1846, found the people of the new village growing wheat and maize and three kinds of peas and beans. In the gardens there were watermelons and *spanspek* (cantaloupes), vegetables, fruit trees and vineyards with rows 600 metres long. Small patches of cotton were grown successfully in Lydenburg – and so it should have been, for this Bushveld is the original home of all the world's cotton.

It is one of the strangest mysteries of a mysterious country, for woven cotton, preserved in a silver jar dating back to 3 000 B.C., has been discovered at Mohenjo-Daro in West Pakistan. Yet Sir Joseph Hutchinson, from evidence based on the genetics of the plant, argues that cotton which has the linting gene that enables it to be spun could only have come from the wild species of the arid Bushveld of southern Africa. So it appears that while the country around Ohrigstad and Lydenburg was

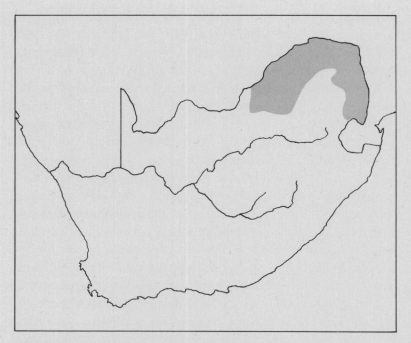

The Bushveld.

still in the Stone Age, there were people who carried cotton with them up Africa, to India and across the oceans to Peru. But at its birthplace cotton never became a crop of great importance. The bread-eaters again wanted wheat more than anything else the soil could produce and by 1848 they had even succeeded in erecting a water-mill to grind the grain. The tables were stacked with bread smeared with mutton fat, and venison. Beef and poultry were regarded as delicacies, because the palate soon tires of wild meat.

But cultivation of the Bushveld was not on a large enough scale to destroy the habitat of the tsetse, and the cattle still died while their owners went down with the fever. Combined with the fact that the elephants had become gun shy and moved off into Mozambique, the prospects were so grim that a migration away from the Bushveld began in 1870. Some went back to the Highveld and others went west to drier country. In 1848 Potgieter himself had moved once again to begin yet another new town to the west of the present-day Louis Trichardt. But the old fighter, one of the founders of the Transvaal Republic, would still lead many a commando in battle before he lay on his last sick-bed with a Dutch hymn as his muttered prayer:

De Heer zal op mijn smeeken
Geen hulp mij doen ontbreken
Hy houdt getrouw zijn woord . . .

It was a deep faith in a divine destiny, and it soared higher than the determinism of science. Only men such as he could have vanquished the Matabele and Zulu, tamed the wide expanses of the Highveld and endured the fevers of the bush country. He died on Heroes' Day, the 16th December 1852 – the day that later came to be called the Day of the Covenant.

When the evacuation began, many such pioneer graves were left in the little cemeteries shaded by spreading camelthorns, great wild figs with crowns like cathedral domes, and fantastic baobabs, their bare branches like skeleton arms. But the retreat was not a surrender. The toughest Bushvelders remained and so did the poorest, who were unable to buy land on the Highveld where a man could no longer ride a horse for four hours along the sides of a square to become the owner of a farm. Many of them eked out a meagre living by exploiting another natural resource of the Bushveld, its trees. The acacias and the silver-grey boekenhout became firewood; the apiesdoring supplied poles for the fences that the Highveld farmers were erecting; and the trunks of the ornate cussonias, with crowns like huge cabbages, became brake-blocks for the wagons. Some Bushvelders became craftsmen and made furniture from kiaat and tambotie, wood as finely grained as brown onyx. The delicate fragrance of tambotie, which it never loses, was like an incense, reminding those who know the Bushveld of the fever and the suffering of the people.

Until as recently as the first two decades of the 20th century they were a forgotten people, the pariahs of a land to which the rich men of the grasslands came down in winter. Their only monument is a book, written by that great Afrikaner poet, Dr C. Louis Leipoldt, to tell of their suffering and their courage. In one of his poems he, too, echoes the faith of Potgieter:

Moed, mense, hou moed:
Die kwaad sal verander in goed –
Die môrelig kom uit die duister.

It is an exhortation for the Afrikaner people to have courage; for good comes out of evil, as the dawn follows the night.

For a while it seemed as if there would be a new dawn over the Bushveld – the golden dawn of nuggets, glistening faintly in the clear streams. Far away in the west, right on the edge of the Great Thirstland, a little gold had been mined at Tati. Then, Edward Button, a prospector from Natal, panned alluvial gold and crushed a reef at Eersteling, near Marabastad – another of the Bushveld towns where the pioneers had endured so much. Two years later there were more finds, on the farms Geelhoutboom and Graskop, to the east of Lydenburg.

People without money to buy either lead or gunpowder from the *smouse,* the travelling traders, gossiped wildly about pans full of nuggets bigger than peas. The temperature of a new fever, gold fever, rose when the first public goldfield in the Transvaal was proclaimed by the Volksraad in May 1873. In the Lydenburg district the price of a farm, which could have been bought before the discovery for R300, rose to R18 000. Road-building began between the fields and Pretoria and Delagoa

Bay in the east. On another notable Heroes' Day, December 16th 1874, Burgers, the President of the Republic, came to Lydenburg and bought the famous Perseverance Nugget. From it the first gold coinage of the South African Republic was minted – the sovereign named after him and now so highly prized by numismatists.

But the Bushvelders saw few of the sovereigns. The goldfields were petering out and it seemed that the malaria mosquitoes, now stinging the fortune-hunters as well as the farmers, would soon rule the bush once more. But then hopes revived with another discovery to the south of Lydenburg, towards the land of the Swazis, in a valley between the Drakensberg and Lebombo ranges. This place came to be known as De Kaap (the Cape), although it was a hell-hole of heat with not an oak or a white gabled house in sight. The discovery was made by G. M. Moodie, a man helping to plan a different kind of progress for the Transvaal. He had been instructed by that forgotten man of vision of South African history, President Thomas Francois Burgers, to survey a railway line to Delagoa Bay and to form a company in England to build it. Today that railway runs through another valley, where a green dawn broke over the Bushveld – the thriving 19 000 hectares of irrigated farmland along the Crocodile River Valley, and one of the show-places of South Africa's modern agricultural system.

Moodie's field was 'rushed' in 1884; and the gold-mining town of Barberton soon became as loud and bawdy as any group of miners, many of whom had panned in California and Australia, could make it. This was one Bushveld town where no hymns were sung at the christening. Within two years those miners were raising the roof and drinking a toast in champagne to the barmaids and the great new Witwatersrand Goldfields. Greed, like a falconer, had drawn the fortune-hunters from the hot Bushveld valleys to the Highveld; and his golden lure lay in the conglomerate of the ridges where the white waters had invited the first Voortrekkers – the Meyers, the Oosthuizens and the Bezuidenhouts – to sow wheat.

Yet Barberton basked and prospered, and still produces some gold from historic old mines like Sheba, Moodie's and Consort. It looks up to the mists, high up on its mountains, where a new fortune, great forests of pine trees, is ready to be processed. But it, too, is a town of memories rather than of visions. And in the cavalcade of its past the most daring riders were the men who took the transport wagons across the Lowveld down to Delagoa Bay. They were guided over the rolling plain by the ancient granite kopjes, the inselbergs, which rose above a country where the landscape had been gouged out of the Drakensberg by erosion down to the oldest rocks known to man, the very foundation of the earth on which he lives; and in the black cherts of the mountains the oldest known fossils – blue-green algae and bacteria – close to the very beginning of life on this planet, have been found. Like the members of the Trichardt trek, the transport riders were plagued from outspan to outspan by fever and the fly. The story of their adventures and hardships will live as long as people read 'Jock of the Bushveld'.

But a new Great Trek was beginning to inspan to conquer the Bushveld world of insects. It was manned by men who 'bundu bashed' in trucks and were armed with microscopes. Science had already discovered how the two most important vectors of malaria in southern Africa, *Anopheles gambiae* and *A. funestus*, carry the disease to man. At first the attempt was made to keep the insect away from its human prey by building houses that, with their screened windows and doors, were like a new kind of *laager*. Some of the farmers took quinine till their ears were always humming, but others were too poor to buy it. There was not even enough money to distribute it free in schools. Dr Leipoldt complained: 'The Bushveld community has come to accept malaria as an ever-present, almost inevitable accompaniment of life . . .'

The State was shocked into action by an epidemic during which 'a dead native was taken almost every day from every hut'. As Minister of Health in 1929, Dr D. F. Malan appointed a world authority on the disease, Professor N. H. Swellengrebel, to find out whether malaria could be combated here as elsewhere. Field entomologists had already been studying the bionomics of the mosquito– where it lived, how it bred and how it fed. They found that it was most vulnerable in the larval stage. Armed with little more than used motor-oil to spray the streams and wet areas, a magnificent campaign of destruction was waged by Dr D. H. S. Anneke from his headquarters laboratory at Tzaneen. It was an epic of preventive medicine, accomplished with a small staff and little money. But the real break-through only came during World War II with the discovery of new and mighty weapons such as DDT and pyrethrum aerosols and the preventive drug, Atabrin. Science defeated but did not destroy the mosquito. In the new, vital, prosperous Bushveld it still has its lairs and the Bushvelders are ever-vigilant for its attacks in the wet seasons.

The tsetse fly, like the magnificent flora of the Bushveld, became a victim of progress as its habitat was destroyed. Where tough pockets persisted, the fly was attacked with DDT. In the Lowveld of faraway Maputaland, between the Lebombo Mountains and the Indian Ocean, the bush was sprayed from the air. But ecologists fear that DDT, an indiscriminate killer, may have harmed the useful insects as much as the foes of man and his animals. However, the poverty-stricken Tsonga people can own cattle again; they no longer carry so many dead from their huts; and the soil lies waiting to receive irrigation water from the J. G. Strydom Dam in the gorge of the Pongola River.

In the north, where a small enclave of a truly tropical climate thrusts across the Limpopo River, experts in animal husbandry, planning huge cattle ranches for the more arid regions inside the frost-free belt, opened a research station. The tsetse had been virtually beaten, but there was a new enemy – the sweltering heat which made it impossible for better breeds of cattle from cold climates to thrive here. Yet science would triumph again. Prospecting among the genes of the different herds, the agriculturists produced another successful Bushvelder, the Bonsmara breed of cattle.

There are still many problems of erosion, bush encroachment, droughts and water supplies ahead, but South Africans are proud of their work – accomplished without foreign aid in money or expertise – to make the Bushveld one of the greatest ranching areas of Africa, and a source of meat protein for the country's growing population.

Below the grass of its ranches and the soils of the irrigated lands, the Bushveld hides other treasures – its wealth of base minerals. Even the children at the old alluvial diggings had looked for nuggets in the streams, but the new wealth, which hid itself and assumed many forms, was hard to identify. That is why apatite, which varies in colour from white to brown, green, yellow and violet, takes its name from the Greek word meaning 'to deceive'; and it has come to play a vital role in the future agricultural development of South Africa. The challenge, the excitement and adventure of finding this and other minerals, produced other famous Bushveld characters – the old prospectors. They wandered with ox wagons and pack-donkeys from the Blouberg, along the Soutpansberg to the Drakensberg, where lovely Mariepskop, a scenic gem of the Bushveld, towers above the Lowveld. They dreamed of a rich find and when they thought that they had made it, many of them turned back to Tzaneen to show it to 'the doctor' to make sure what it was. The doctor was Dr Hans Merensky, the fabulously wealthy discoverer of the diamond on the west coast of South Africa and in Namibia, who now lived on his estate, Westphalia, experimenting with conservation methods to improve Bushveld farming.

It was a kind of pilgrimage that the old prospectors made to him, bringing as votive offerings their samples which were placed in small heaps all round the *stoep* (verandah) of the big farmhouse. In this way the web of trails of the prospectors and the geological knowledge of the doctor led to the discovery of Phalaborwa at the foot of the lonely Loolekop. Here there is a 11 km² volcanic pipe, in which the boiling lava mixed an incredible wealth and variety of base minerals. Ultimately its copper-mine will be one of the biggest open-cast mines in the world. The apatite alone gives South Africa an assured supply of half a million tonnes of rock phosphate a year for another 150 years. From this gaping hole in the Bushveld there will come fertilizers to help sustain the fertility of the Highveld's vast fields of maize. And Phalaborwa will become a great Bushveld city.

Most of this land below the Highveld plateau was in the 'White Horseshoe', the depopulated area left by the wars of the blacks. When the first Voortrekkers moved in they were unaware that it was a treasure chest of minerals, only to be discovered by professional prospectors. Undoubtedly their richest find was made in the Bushveld Igneous Complex, a huge assemblage of once-molten rocks. In addition to platinum, there are reserves of chromite that may soon make South Africa the world's largest producer of ferrochrome. The Timeball Hill series, an iron formation, outcrops for hundreds of kilometres and was already a source of ore for the first Iron Age smiths. Part of this wealth now falls within the borders of a new black independent Homeland, Bophuthatswana, which is training men for technical tasks, including those of mine managers and company directors.

The archaeologists and anthropologists, as well as the geological Voortrekkers of science, are discovering hidden treasures in the Bushveld. Their work is another remarkable trek – a journey of exploration into the past. And the Bushveld is old, very old. Here the earliest men able to make bone tools may have lived and hunted a million years ago; and on the banks of the Limpopo River the men of the Iron Age first tilled the soil with hoes and built their capital, Mapungubwe, on top of a flat sandstone hill. They, too, treasured gold and made of it beads and a sceptre and rhinoceros for their ruler.

The Bushveld slumbered for centuries, while the black man made war and died of malaria. But they, too, are farming irrigated lands and preparing to work a copper-mine of their own. At Phalaborwa, where their ancestors beat out hoes and assegais on a stone anvil, they now drive the big tipper trucks that pour thousands of tonnes of ore a day into the giant crushers.

The new Bushveld, from the Crocodile to the Letaba Rivers, has become alive with enterprise. The energy of the Bushvelders is no longer sapped by a war against enemy insects; and as they work and multiply they boast that the men of the Highveld Eldorado will yet learn to doff their hats to the people who conquered the sub-tropical lands below the *berg*.

7

Words at work

The paper he delivered was concerned with adding up, collecting and spending vast sums of money. The Minister of Finance of the newly independent Republic of Transkei was presenting his budget to parliament – one of the most intricate financial processes of a modern state. Between him and the great black chiefs, who had made treaties with the British Government by signing with a crudely drawn cross, there was a time gap of 125 years – five generations during which the Nguni, Sotho and other African tongues, wending their way through the mazes of syntax and orthography, had become written languages: and the hand that initially guided the pen was white.

When the treaties were made in 1844 a copy, written in his own language, was also given to the chief. This was possible because the missionaries had listened to the people speaking, made word lists with their meanings, and then discovered how the noun-prefix colours the entire structure of the Bantu sentence. The Rev. James Archbell, retreating before the warring tribes, still found time to set up a small printing press on the north bank of the Vaal River. With his own hands he selected the letters from a small font of type and watched the lines growing slowly in the composing stick. From them there came his *Grammar of the Bechuana Language*, completed in 1826.

But Robert Moffat performed one of the most stupendous literary labours in the history of South Africa. Once he had learned to speak the language, he began to translate the Bible into Sechuana (Tswana). Often he sat in his tent writing by the light of a lantern as he trekked by wagon as far as the new kraal of Mzilikazi in Rhodesia. The Old Testament, from Genesis to Kings, was printed at the Kuruman Mission Station in 1853. The great task, including the New Testament, was completed during the next four years. The Word, the tales of the shepherds and hunters and warriors of another desert country, could now be brought to the people of this arid thornveld in their own language.

The sensitive men listening to the people as they talked heard music-like sounds as the gong beats of the rich vowels vibrated over the staccato rhythm of the sentences. They realised that these were beautiful languages for the orator and the preacher.

And the African tongues were a practical tool for the first farmers who used black workers. Their herdsmanship was a skill which was only of value if they understood orders, because the animal husbandry methods of the white man were different and better. The blacks soon had to learn how to handle a wagon and its team of oxen, then a plough, a planter, a cultivator, a wheat harvester – and today they drive 250 000 tractors on the maize farms of the Highveld.

In varying degrees the one group learned the language of the other. Most of Natal's farmers have long been able to give orders in Zulu; the eastern Free Staters were fluent in Southern Sotho, the language of Moshweshwe; and in the Transvaal the miners evolved a lingua franca, Fanagalo, with which all the migrant tribesmen, from the Zambesi's source to the Ciskei, became familiar. Without Fanagalo at the rock-face the bars of gold could not have left the refinery.

In the Cape, as the Hottentots were absorbed, their language disappeared, leaving only vestiges in the vocabulary of the region, especially in many of the plant names still in common use. Van Riebeeck's Hottentot interpreters, Eva and her uncle, Harry, were the means by which the gap between the Germanic gutturals and the volley of click sounds was bridged. At first it was the language of the hard bargain, the peace talk – and then of domestic and agricultural labour. But an old Hottentot vocabulary, probably compiled by George Frederick Wreede, suggests that during the 17th century the Dutch made some effort to study the complex language of the tribes that came to graze and barter cattle on the slopes of Table Mountain above Van Riebeeck's first fort.

In addition to learning by personal contact there was the process of formal education provided by schools – hundreds of mission schools that began when the first, which was exclusively for black children, was opened at the Cape in 1791.

But education is such a powerful instrument of political policy that controversy about its philosophy and content was inevitable. It was the aim of the missions to impart a culture that was a reflection of European ideals – if somewhat blurred. For instance, in 1864 Lovedale College, the first institution to train black missionaries and teachers, required its senior students to study – in addition to training of a more practical nature – a chapter of the Greek Testament, an ode of Anacreon and the first book of the Aeneid.

To many it seemed remote from the kind of world into which the students would walk – and far removed from the ideas of the men who had first translated the Bible into Tswana. But several changes in emphasis and syllabus were to follow changes in policies and ideas. Dr C. T. Loram, in 1921, recommended that instruction in the schools should take more account of the culture of the blacks and provide separate curricula that would fit them for their life-work. Even then educated black leaders resisted the change, which they interpreted as an attempt merely to make them more economically useful in the service of the whites. At one time they were accused of wanting to produce a nation of imitation Europeans, forgetting all that was beautiful in African tradition, custom, history, folklore, music and art; but in the final analysis vernacular education has been rejected by South African blacks because of its isolationist implications.

One of the main features of black education has been an upsurge, like a tidal wave of ambition, of the black parents' desire to send their children to school, where they will not only reap the knowledge of Western civilization but acquire the ability to seek greater job opportunities.

But the choice of the kind of education the blacks now get was made for them in 1954 by the Nationalist Government. And so the black children, who often walk for miles across the hills of the Homelands or along the streets of the townships to get to school, are first taught their mother tongue. Afrikaans and English come later as separate subjects, to prepare the child to face a bilingual white society, but at secondary school level the question of the medium of instruction (English or Afrikaans) has become a highly contentious issue.

In 1976 about 75 per cent of black children were attending school – a total of 4 000 000 between the ages of seven and 14. On the other hand, only three out of every ten black children who enter secondary school matriculate and a mere trickle of potential graduates go on to college.

A feature of the demographic structure of the rapidly-increasing black society is that 28 per cent of the population is composed of children of school-going age, whereas in western developed countries it is 21 per cent. More important, in terms of South Africa, is the projection that by the year 2 000 there will be 7 000 000 black children at school – more than the estimated white population. What is more, over 10 000 new teachers will be required each year in black schools to meet the rapid increase expected in the number of pupils.

In 1976 Soweto erupted onto the headlines of the world and the touchstone of conflict was 'Bantu education' – a system devised solely for the blacks and one seen to be inferior. A uniform system of education is now being demanded as a top priority. South Africa has been presented with realities that must be acknowledged and met if the black man is to achieve a transition comparable with that of the Afrikaners themselves, who have adapted within the past five decades to the age of technology and science.

At first the evolution of Afrikaans had been as unconscious as the growth of an embryo. The Company, more intent on profits than on cultural achievement, had failed to provide the schools that might have preserved the flexional forms of Dutch. In the life of the *trekboere*, the *grensboere* and the Voortrekkers there were no grammar books or dictionaries – only the Bible, which kept them anchored to Dutch. But the idiom of the veld began to break the rules with phonetic and structural changes that heralded a new language, just as Dutch itself had discarded the sound-shift and the elaborate battery of flexions in High German.

Afrikaans came to be spoken long before it was written. But there was a consciousness of 'nationhood' even during the period of dichotomy between spoken Afrikaans and written Dutch. Men began to say of themselves: 'I am an Afrikaner.' In the calm Paarl Valley the spirit suddenly flared up and fused individual patriots into an organised movement, the *Genootskap van Regte Afrikaners* (Society of True Afrikaners). It grew out of a group of men who had been meeting in the parsonage of the Rev. S. J. du Toit, and the official launching date of the Society was the 14th August 1875. The following year Afrikaans began its evolution as a written, printed language when *Die Patriot*, an official organ, was published to spread the message of the main aim: 'To stand up for our Language, our Nation and our Land.' In this little paper also appeared an anthem, written by Arnoldus Pannevis. The verses have long been forgotten by the mass of the people, but they were more than mere christening cups for the new baby. They help to clarify the deep urges of the heart that the poet tried to express – the feeling that every nation has its own country and that for the Afrikaner there would be no other or better destiny than to live on Afrikaner soil. The ships that sailed into Table Bay brought no nostalgia for Holland.

Over a wide geographical area these people had discovered an identity of language and patriotism. But there was also the stimulus of challenge – an official policy aimed at anglicizing the people of the Cape. Later in their history the Afrikaners became convinced that if the blacks did not enjoy 'separate development' within their own social framework and language, they would react as they themselves did when the British tried to make of them a new brand of imperial cultural product, the Anglo-Afrikaner.

In the Cape the emergence of Afrikaans was, therefore, a natural consequence of the physical and psychological environment. But on the distant eastern frontiers, from which so many Voortrekkers came, the process was different in several minor respects. Here the lead came from an English-speaking South African printer and journalist, Louis Meurant, who sensed that the language of the people was no longer Dutch. He concluded that there was no reason why, despite the disparaging names given to '*die taal*' (language), they should be ashamed of it. Fifteen years before *Die Patriot* appeared in Paarl, he began publishing racy satirical dialogues in the *Cradock News*. He called the language used by the two characters, Klaas Waarsegger (Klaas, the truthteller) and Jan Twijfelaar (Jan, the doubter), vernacular Dutch (*plat-Hollandsch*), but it was in fact an early form of Afrikaans – which appeared in print, appropriately enough, as the language of political dispute.

In the two republics north of the Orange River, where educational facilities were limited by lack of finance, Afrikaans was slower to emerge in written form. Here the voice of freedom and of nationalism was the sound of gunfire; and the anthems the commandos sang during both the Wars of Independence were Dutch. But the defiant courage of the north, the deeds of valour and the suffering, became an inspiration to the poets and writers of the south. The military conflict toughened the leaders and in public affairs it produced what has become known as the Age of the Generals. Afrikaners, confident of their growing cultural identity, began the political struggle for the recognition of Afrikaans as the second official language of the Union of South Africa. In this phase of development the political leaders of the north took the most prominent part. But it was not the last stage of the linguistic trek.

Today the Afrikaners themselves speak with pride of 'the wonder of Afrikaans'. English began in the 11th century with the imposition of the language of the Norman-French conquerors on that of the Anglo-Saxon serfs. But Afrikaans bloomed, like a veld flower, not by cross-pollination but as a mutation from Germanic seed, planted in a new soil. English, the vernacular of vernaculars, enriched itself with innovations and borrowings from many languages. And Afrikaans, too, has taken this path.

To protect the young language from needless assimilations, the Afrikaners, like the French in the 17th century, set up an Academy. It made rules of grammar and orthography, published vocabularies and glossaries, and began work on a standard dictionary, *Die Woordeboek van die Afrikaanse Taal*. And the Academy was particularly on guard against the overpowering influence of the English vocabulary, against the hasty incorporation of anglicisms. The procedure did not harm the simplicity of the language of the veld – and some of its greatest works have been its lyric poetry – but it still has to face the challenge of the proliferating terminology of a scientific and technological age. It is not so much a problem of word formation as of numbers – the publication of expensive text-books for a small population. But then all the future problems of South Africa's planners, no matter whether they are putting men or words to work, are essentially problems of numbers.

8

Landscapes of the soul

Southern Africa's great galleries of cave paintings are best viewed through the reverent eyes of an archaeologist-priest, the Abbé Breuil. He regarded the cathedrals of Europe as a revelation of the greatness, the discipline and the sublimity of the up-surging of the ideal of Christian faith in the mediaeval soul; and in the same way the frescoes painted in the rock shelters showed with astonishing freshness the life of hunting peoples who were the sole inhabitants of the mountains for thousands of years before the arrival of the black man, and later, the white.

To him the scenes of living nature on the painted walls did not represent a pictorial game-reserve. He called them 'landscapes of the soul'. With thousands of human figures in the scenes they became a wild paradise, like landscapes seen by man in a dream, expressing throughout *joie de vivre*, the delight of being agile, fleet-footed, supple in sport and dance, deft in shooting arrows. Whether the artist's theme was daily life, hunting, occasionally fishing, or war, the men were in full bodily activity, slim naked bodies, often decorated with bead armlets, anklets and belts. Sometimes the dancers were masked, imitating the eland and other animals, the mantis, insect of magic, or spirits such as Kauha, the Bushman's god. Strange monsters, called 'rain bulls', were connected with rainmaking rites, such as dragging the body of a hippopotamus across dry ground. Then there is also the ballet dance of the harvest, when roots and bulbs are plentiful, and the women set out with their digging sticks.

The pictures soon excited the wonder of the white pioneers and many mysteries and legends were associated with them. Bushmen were supposed to have depicted a unicorn and so it was thought that this animal might actually exist. But Thomas Baines, the famous artist-traveller, and one of the first men to study and copy the cave art, could find no support for the legend. Since then thousands of valleys and mountain slopes have been explored but, although the perfection of line and sense of movement in the paintings have excited great admiration, the unicorn remains only a heraldic emblem.

One of the first to undertake this search was Walter Battiss, the South African artist, who was fascinated by the problems presented by the cave galleries. He believed that there were two distinct styles of art in the rock shelters, beginning with an ancient art, probably thousands of years old, which had much greater aesthetic content than the work of the Bushmen. Some examples of the younger, and cruder, paintings superimposed on the lovely and delicately drawn older work have been found to support that theory. But the actual age, the beginning of this artistic activity, has never been settled, although Lancelot Hogben attempted to draw a conclusion by comparing a bison, painted in the caves of Altamira in Spain about 20 000 years ago when the last great ice age ended, and an eland which appears in a Bushman painting in Lesotho.

However, it is known that the South African Bushmen were painting until quite recently. The pictures in the frescoes tell the story of the arrival of the black man and of warlike feats when poisoned arrows were pitted against assegais as the peaceful little hunters became terrible warriors, defending their territory and the drinking places of the game – until they were exterminated. One of the most recent paintings, in impermanent colours of red ochre, black and white, was found on the farm Klipfontein, near Rouxville in the Orange Free State. It shows two Voortrekkers, the woman in the long dress of that period. The artist had depicted the ultimate conquerors of his people.

But long before it came to admire Bushman paintings, Europe was interested in a different art form – the pictorial reporting of travellers who called at the Cape on their way to the East. People in England first saw the outlines of Table Mountain, with two Hottentots in the foreground, in a book published in 1634 by Thomas Herbert, whose ship called at the Cape when he was on his way to Persia. Many of these drawings, like the tales of the travellers, were rather fanciful. In 1660 Johan Jacobsz Saar must have amazed the directors of the Dutch East India Company by an illustration of Table Bay in his book. It showed the mountain, drawn like a very realistic lion, with the Table floating in the clouds above it. Another German writer, Albrecht Herport, showed Hottentots with entrails of animals strung round their necks; and then, as if this was not startling enough, he added a rhinoceros in armour!

Many of these 17th century pictures are in one or other of South Africa's collections of Africana, and probably the most interesting and valuable items are the water-colours by Hendrik Claudius, in the Johannesburg Africana Museum. Claudius went with Simon van der Stel to Namaqualand in 1685 and painted plants and animals and a few pictures of the famous mountain of copper in that area. He is thus the earliest South African artist whose original work still exists.

But the first South African-born artist was Lady Barrow, a pretty Cape Town girl, Anna Maria Truter, who married the author of *Travels into the Interior of South Africa*. Sir John Barrow's book, published in 1801, is regarded as the most important work written during the first British Occupation of the Cape. His wife was assisted by a professional artist, Samuel Daniell, whose water-colour of the Barrow farmhouse, Buitenzorg, is one of the most familiar Cape landscape paintings.

Dutch houses, fleets of Indiamen at anchor in Table Bay and the Hottentots were favourite subjects of the artists of those years. They are engraved in many minds today as symbols of the beginning of civilisation on these shores. But the botanists and naturalists Masson, Thunberg, Sparrman and the adventurous William Paterson, told the world about a different aspect of the Cape – the beauty of its floral kingdom. And a woodcut of the strange blood flower, a species of *Haemanthus,* was the first picture of the Cape's botanical glory to be seen in Europe. It was made by Mathias de l'Obel, physician to William the Silent and later botanist to James I of England. He had found the remarkable plant growing in Belgium in 1603, the bulbs brought there by ship from the neighbourhood of the Cape of Good Hope.

One of the most eccentric of these 18th century visitors was Francois le Vaillant, who trekked to Namaqualand and across the Orange River. His first two books were published in 1790 and 1795. The Frenchman hunted lion and leopard in a court suit of 'Blue Boy' silk, with white gloves, ostrich-plumed hat, and lace ruffles to show his respect for those noble animals. But as an artist he is remembered for the engravings – in green, blue and black – which appeared in his famous book on birds, *Histoire Naturelle des Oisseaux d'Afrique.* Paris goggled at the remarkable wealth of South Africa's bird life, and snickered at the *risqué* stories of adventures on the trek. But posterity, in spite of what they associate with the names of the nerina trogon and Klaas's cuckoo, is grateful to le Vaillant for a wonderful ornithological record.

The outlines of South African history – and of her geography, botany, zoology and ethnography – emerge more clearly, and with greater artistic merit, from the work of the 19th century explorers who went far inland from the Cape in their wagons. Their illustrations were not great works of art, but they have become Africana, the raw material of the historian. William Burchell, a scientist who sketched with the meticulous accuracy required by his calling, has left many glimpses of memorable scenes – of the rutted wagon-road going north across the Karoo to distant mission stations; of the reed church which Anderson built for the Griquas at Klaarwater; and of a treeless homestead, showing how the sheep farmers lived in 1811.

When Burchell, in the spring of that year, outspanned his

wagons and raised his country's flag on the banks of the Vaal River above its junction with the Orange, it so happened that he was near another great gallery of prehistoric art in southern Africa – the rock engravings scratched deeply with chalcedony or quartz into the glazed dolerite boulders. Among the beautifully drawn outlines of animals there were also symbols, thought to be either an elementary form of writing, hieroglyphs drawn by Bushmen on these stone manuscripts, or else 'title deeds' by means of which the clan leaders showed that certain animals in the territory were their property.

Scores of experts have studied the engravings and disagreed about their purpose and meaning; one of them was even reminded of the Phoenician alphabet. Some of the compositions were elaborate landscapes with grass, trees and termite mounds in the foreground, men hunting animals in the middle distance, and stars in the background – although the moon was never shown.

Much less puzzling records of the life of veld and bush were contained in the book in which Captain Cornwallis Harris was able to use lithographs to reproduce his illustrations. Before 1830 most of the travellers had been limited to aquatints to make their work more widely known. In his *Portraits of the Game and Wild Animals of Southern Africa,* first published in India in 1838, Harris included a full-length portrait of Mzilikazi – a tall, pot-bellied figure, almost naked, accompanied by his Chanter of the King's Praises as he walked past the circular kraal of beehive grass huts.

Harris also met the Voortrekkers on the plains of the Orange Free State. But he made no sketches or water-colour portraits of their leaders, possibly because they refused to sit for him. It is known that Hendrik Potgieter adhered so rigidly to the Second Commandment that he would not have his portrait painted. But in any case Harris was more interested in the unusual landscape, the herds of game, the hunting of the buffalo and the elephant, than he was in the small band of white men and their wagons, although he was later to write one of the first histories of the Voortrekkers and champion their cause.

And the southern African landscape would dominate the art of the country long after the travellers who were merely using brush and pencil to report on what they had seen, had become commonplace. Three decades after Harris had crossed the veld, a young herdboy, J. E. A. Volschenk, began to make pictures with coloured chalks on stones in the Riversdale district; and when he had learned to paint in oils, he depicted the magnificence of the scene around him.

Similar landscapes in the Worcester Valley exerted their influence on Hugo Naude, who was born in 1869, 16 years after Volschenk. But his style bore the stamp of the Post-Impressionists and he described the beauty of the world around him in a free and unimpassioned manner.

Then, at the beginning of the next century, a young Hollander, Pieter Wenning, came to South Africa, and although his style was less advanced than that of Naude, his reputation soon outstripped that of the group of artists then beginning to form in Cape Town. Another Hollander, Frans Oerder, dominated the art world of the Transvaal until the great Hendrik Pierneef appeared to lend magic to the trees of the Bushveld, which he sketched minutely before he put a brush to canvas.

Up to 1940 the Cape remained the artistic centre of South Africa and it was dominated by two women, Irma Stern and Maggie Laubscher, who introduced Expressionism to these shores. But one thing these South African artists shared with those before them and those who followed – an enduring fascination with their environment, irrespective of painting trends and influences.

The so-called New Group was started in Cape Town in 1938 and one of the founders, Gregoire Boonzaier, introduced a more robust quality into the descriptive manner of the Cape painters. Not to be outdone, Pretoria, on the border between the Bushveld and the Highveld hills where the Bushmen painted, produced Walter Battiss, who had been moved early on in his life by a study of the rock artists. Alexis Preller, also of Pretoria, produced work in which the themes and symbols were suggestively African; and in the north these two painters have dominated the art scene since World War II.

But the galleries of Johannesburg, where art has the advantage of wealthy patronage, are now crowded with the works of a coming generation of Abstract Expressionists. The objective world, which so many of the famous artists attempted to portray, has become as ephemeral as a dream. However, this style may only mark an outspan, not the end of the journey of exploration of South Africa's landscape painters.

As the artistic trek moves on from exhibition to exhibition, it may, in the distant future, see the emergence of an indigenous art, less concerned with objective nature, but inspired by delving deeply into the spirit world of the tribal subconscious: like Credo Mutwa's portrayal of one of the genesis myths of his people.

Unlike the Africans of the Congo, the black peoples south of the Limpopo River did not make wood carvings. But the women did scratch decorative designs with amazing trueness of line on their clay pots – chevrons, inverted hatched triangles and occasionally rectangles and diamonds; and similar designs were later smeared on hut walls. There was not much time for art in the struggle for existence – the artistic impulse was directed into functional channels. In the biological sense it is an overflow of excess energy, a special form of constructive play. The black man found this outlet mainly in song and dance. It was an escape from the material struggle, opening the doors to a fantastic world of super-reality – boasts about the prowess of the hunter, the bravery of the warrior in battle or the cajolery of lovers.

This does not mean that there is no modern black art. And there is cross-pollination of ideas and influences between Africa and Europe; the process is at work and has already produced painters and sculptors of great promise, such as Sydney Kumalo and Lucas Sithole. The luminescence of a handful of gems may yet reveal the hidden wealth of a mine from which new concepts of beauty could emerge.

9

Nature's chord

The bronze bust of Shaka stands there on its pedestal, like a ghostly, immobile conductor of an American Negro jazz band. A young Zulu, who has never thrown an assegai, walks past, armed with a transistor radio tuned in to Radio Bantu. It sheds saxophone notes, like falling leaves, onto the dusty streets of Stanger, which Shaka had called *kwaDukuza,* 'the place of the wanderer', when he settled there in 1826 to pick the fruits of victory – fat steaks, beer and courtiers to sing the sweetest song of all, the praises of the king. The jazz fades out and a taped commercial, an electronic ghost, chants the praises of a detergent – universal cleanser for a tarnished age. The bronze image seems to vibrate, to shake with anger, in the sound waves.

But the next programme is music that Shaka would have understood. There is the rhythm, the resonant harmony and the faint lilt of the simple melody of a song from the valleys, sung by a school choir of Zulu children. It had been put together, like a broken work of sculpture, from fragments of sound that were heard in *kwaDukuza* in the days before the assassins, Mhlangane and Dingane, drove their assegais into Shaka's side and he died, screaming for mercy. Then there were calm moments in tribal life, filled with the songs of the love dances, the *iJadu,* when the young men met the maidens on the veld to select wives; the lively overture, the *iNkondola;* and the solemn clan anthems, the *iHubo,* sung as the warriors raised their shields in salute: forgotten songs of long ago.

White musicians and anthropologists have been delving with tape recorders into this musical past of the black man, recording the songs that only the old people can recall. And the powerful medium of the radio is bringing them back to the grass huts of the hill country and the cement-block houses of the townships. It has created a new opportunity for black talent to express itself, for the music of many peoples to cross thresholds which might otherwise be barred. The contacts, and the challenge, of this territory of sounds are patterned, like the geographical mosaic, and will retain the cultural distinctiveness of one of the unique treasures of southern Africa.

To a lesser extent than song, instrumental music is also a part of this wealth. Vasco da Gama described in his log-book how he listened to a Hottentot band when he landed at Mossel Bay on the 2nd December 1497. They were playing reed flutes, closed at one end, and sounded by blowing across the open end. But they had not yet discovered the secret of the Greek pan-pipes – joining together reeds of different pitches to make an instrument on which one man could play a tune. So the Hottentot flute band consisted of a number of men, each blowing a pipe of different length. The tribes also had the *gora,* a stringed instrument sounded by wind – and probably the last genuine Korana Hottentot to play on it was old Mulukab who performed for Professor Percival R. Kirby in 1942 when he was busy with his extensive studies of African music.

It is the twang of the plucked bowstring that gives the Bushman his music. This sound is not merely a single note but a complete natural chord, the chord which has given rise to the modern art of harmony. But the faint twang needs to be amplified by a sound-box. In the Kalahari today Bushmen can still be seen holding a bow to their mouths while they tap the string with a dry grass stalk. In this way, by using nature's chord, they are able to play tunes that sound like bugle calls. This ancient music, that used to delight Greek archers in the time of Homer, can still be heard in the shade of the camelthorn trees when the small groups of desert people rest during the heat of the noon-day sun.

The musical instruments of the native peoples – the Bushmen, the Hottentots and the black man – have been grouped by experts as follows: rattles and clappers; drums; xylophones; *sansas* – tiny keyboard instruments with iron tongues; 'bull-roarers' and spinning discs; horns and trumpets; whistles and flutes, including the reed flute bands; and that stringed wind instrument, the *gora,* which is peculiar to the Hottentots and unique to southern Africa. Except for the *sansa,* which is found among the Venda of the Northern Transvaal where the Iron Age dawned, metal was not used in the making of musical instruments.

Southern Africa was never a mute world where only the roar of the lion, the barking of jackals and the clash of antelope horns locked in combat could be heard. The sounds of man-made music floated down from the sandstone krantzes or rose up from the bush for thousands of years; and travellers through the Homelands, who listen carefully, will hear more than the hymns that are sung in little mission churches. Along the foothills of the Maluti Mountains old Sotho women still tap the *molopa,* a drum made from clay, at the initiation ceremony of the girls. There are trumpet blowers, who have made their *ixilongo* from lengths of reed and the horn of an ox – crude

imitations of the bugles they heard sounding the reveille as dawn broke over British army camps. There are lovelorn maidens playing the *iugube,* a mouth-resonated stringed instrument which gives out the same sounds as a Jew's-harp. And there are daydreaming youths, who produce fairy-like music in two-part harmony from a *zambi,* the string of which is made from palm leaf.

It is only in the hot country of the Soutpansberg that the traveller might hear the deep boom of the great tribal drums of the Venda, the *ngoma,* that are played on ceremonial occasions. The Voortrekkers under Trichardt and Potgieter listened to them with awe, wondering what they might portend. Here, too, there is the tinkling of the *mbila,* the calabash-resonated xylophone, but it is such a precious tribal possession that each of them, rarely for sale, is valued at the price of an ox. This is the instrument with which tourists have become most familiar, because the Tsonga play them at the 'war dances' which are held in the compounds of Johannesburg's gold mines. It came to *iGoli,* the Golden City, in ancient dhows, canoes and rafts, possibly even on the backs of lurching camels, and then down Africa. The trail has been traced back to Malaysia, which was also the first home of the oboe-like instruments that are played under palm trees on the East Coast, from Mombasa to Somalia.

Other Malay music also came to the Cape straight across the Indian Ocean in slave ships, brought out by people whose language became a kind of Malay-Afrikaans. They loved the old folk-songs – their own and those of the Dutch – for instance, the story of the little prince, *Al is ons Prinsje nog zo Klein.* They had choirs at picnics who sang *ghommaliedjies,* gay simple little tunes that soon set feet a-dancing. Weddings were another occasion for choral performances, but for the choirs the climax was reached during Carnival Time between Christmas and New Year's Day. Although the music is different, the East and West and black Africa all have their own versions of the Feast of the First Fruits. But the Malays had no pipe-organ music. Their instruments were of the simplest kind. An old drawing, kept in an album by Lady D'Urban, the Cape Governor's wife, shows two Malay couples dancing to a three-piece 'orchestra' – a drum, a home-made guitar and that oboe-like instrument that the black man copied long before he reached South Africa.

In spite of Islam, there remained in the life of the Cape Malays the mystical rite of the *Khalifa.* Spectators watched with awe the swaying of the drum-players pounding on the *rabannas* while songs were intoned in Arabic. Incense wreathed the dancers in a swirling mist, and when the desired state of hypnotic ecstasy was reached they hacked at their arms with swords and thrust skewers through their legs, cheeks and shoulders. It was a witness to the power of faith – and possibly some very skilled swordplay.

Quite different in its artistic form and evolution is the Coon

Carnival which the Cape coloured people stage during the New Year. It is a *pot-pourri* of sound, colour and movement that has been mixed in the earthy jar of Cape Town's culture – a heritage of the taverns where the sailors sang, the American film world, Dutch and Malay folk music, and dancing that belongs to Africa as much as to the age of the Charleston. But it is an expression of distinctiveness, of group pride. Even if the colourful spectacle has components which have been borrowed from far and wide, it is like the first rough sketch on a canvas that may, in the course of time, become a finished composition. The Carnival is the music and dance of the masses. But their inherent talent has also manifested itself by achievements in the world of Western ballet and opera.

And Western music in southern Africa is still like the first movement of a symphony in sonata form, an announcement of the principal subject – the classical bonds with Europe – with a bridge forming slowly to open the road to free fantasia, the development of themes with characteristic rhythmic and melodic features. It is mainly the status-music of the concert halls, competing with the cacophony of the hit parades, the radio and the discotheques.

But the music of Africa has clearly developing new themes; there is the vibrant music of the townships – music developed in America and brought back to Africa from where it originated; and then already heard in orchestrated form there is *boere-musiek* – songs and dances that go back to the days of the *trekboere,* when the violin, the guitar and the concertina were played in the *hartbeeshuis.*

But it was the Calvinistic psalms of the Sabbath, of morning and evening devotions in the farmhouse, that had the most important conditioning effect on the ear of the Afrikaners. They are sung like anthems – prayers for guidance and strength in this land of infinite diversity, where destiny has moulded a new people to rock the cradles with their own lullaby, the *wiegeliedjie,* to mourn with undaunted faith at the graveside, and to sing with pride the majestic national anthem, *Die Stem van Suid-Afrika.*

IO

Green horizons

The sower of seed in the black Highveld turf may find joy in the gold and green of a crop ripening in the autumn sunlight, but for the herdsman there is no earthly bliss equal to the sight of Afrikander cattle grazing quietly in rich veld, no sound as sweet as the lowing of cows when they come back to their calves in the kraal. It is a feeling that goes far deeper than the mere greed of ownership or the pride of the possessor of wealth.

Men must have felt like this since Neolithic times, when they settled below the fountain of Jericho, or caught the new-born of wild cattle and taught them to follow the Mongol nomads of the *steppes.* The domestication of animals has left its spoors in all human hearts. And the people of southern Africa, both black and white, responded to this primitive call, this voice of the earth and its plants and animals.

But for them farming will soon cease to be a way of life – a harvesting of the bounty of the soil, the satisfaction of the bumper crop and the despair of the drought years, but a good life for all that. Farming must become the food production industry, the agribusiness of America, as efficient as any production line. But it will not be a push-button transition. Nature works in long shifts – the slow march of the seasons, the rise and fall of the sun from the summer to the winter solstice, the birth and death of generations.

The development from the first Cape ploughman's team of oxen to the tractor has taken ten generations; and within the lifetime of the next two, South Africa must assemble a new agricultural machine to feed 70 000 000 people. Some of the parts will be brand new, and others as old as the wagon or the wooden plough. The efficiency of the workers will differ at first according to where they operate – the peasant plots of the Homelands and the factory farms of the whites. But it will level out gradually for skill, like labour, migrates across borders to answer the call of necessity.

Missionaries took the lead with the gift of a plough, but the first move by a Cape government to teach the blacks a new form of agriculture was made in 1825 when potatoes and green vegetables were introduced into Western Kaffraria. There were experiments with many new crops, including indigo, coffee and tobacco, and a private trader named Beattie even introduced silkworms from Japan in the Elliotdale District, where mulberries grow luxuriantly.

None of the results were as spectacular as, for instance, the arrival of pineapple cultivation in Hawaii. The blacks remained fortified behind a wall of tradition, surrounded by a moat of magical fertility rites. In the little fields the women planted the maize, millet and sorghum they knew, while the men herded cattle or sat drinking beer in the shade of a hut. Unlike the more settled Chinese peasant, their system of shifting agriculture could not realise the value of animal manure, and for many years the chemical fertilizers of the white farmers were regarded as *muti* (medicine), as just another kind of magic.

The industrious Fingoes were the first black people to learn that the different agricultural methods of the white man actually yielded substantial results in practice. They went to work for the farmers, particularly in the Somerset East district, and by so doing they broke a psychological barrier and introduced a new idea into their world. For the first time in their long history it became known that a man could leave his kraal to sell his labour for goods or for money.

Before that in traditional black society no man, except for enslaved Bushmen, had worked for a master. The chief allocated a piece of tribal land to him when he married and the women grew the crops. Cattle were their capital and status symbols, and they gave no thought to accumulating a large reserve of grain. After a good harvest, they did not work the next year; if there was a crop failure, they knew that the neighbours would help; and if the plight was general, the *impis* went out to plunder tribes that lived where the rains had fallen.

Then the Fingoes learned to inspan a team of oxen to a wagon or a plough; they saw maize planted in rows to make it easier to weed the lands; they used a spade to turn irrigation water from the canals into the beds; and they sowed wheat and ate bread.

In 1865 the Government settled a large number of Fingoes in the Transkei and they brought with them not only the farming knowledge of Somerset East but a new domesticated animal, the sheep. Soon there were 1 733 ploughs and 440 wagons in Fingoland and by 1879 the wool clip of 211 174 sheep brought a cash income to spend at the trading stores.

It was the lure of money rather than the ideal of good husbandry or the care of the soil which made other people follow their example. The emporia of the bush, the 'Kaffir Truck Stores' as they were known, not only satisfied old needs but created new ones that could be fulfilled in exchange for golden sovereigns, old Rijksdaalders, worn 'tickeys', blackened copper coins – or a chicken, a bucketful of maize or a bag of wool.

The economic history of the black man could be written from the stock sheets of these stores that had a kind of universal advertising slogan – *Goedkoop Winkel:* Bargain Store. The stoep was the show window with usually a row of three-legged cast-iron pots of different sizes, and coils of shiny copper wire. The dark interior was a kind of fairyland of the heart's desire – the rainbow hues of woollen blankets, cotton prints from Manchester, shoes for the women and boots for the men to bring the agony of fashion to calloused feet, khaki trousers and that ultimate status symbol of dress, the ready-made suit.

Only a long, dirty counter separated the soft goods department from the groceries. Here were the new foods for which the blacks had developed a taste in the kitchens of the farmers – sugar, sweets, coffee, tea, tins of sardines and white bread. Each sale was an ordeal of patience for the storekeeper as the customers eyed and felt each article in a timeless daze of fantasy. The closing of a deal was signified by the inevitable request for a *bonsella,* a handful of peppermints or boiled sweets.

Many of the wood-and-iron buildings of the old traders have disappeared from the South African landscape, or given place to the chain stores of the village, but they were the original stimulus to the birth of a money economy among the blacks of the Homelands. They were, too, an index of the standard of living of the people and of two of the great transitions in their lives – the sale of their labour and the need to get away from mere subsistence farming to the production of a surplus for exchange. Not only were more ploughs, planters, harrows and cultivators sold to those who wanted to stay and cultivate the land, but in the course of time there came the bicycle to give added mobility to the migrating labourers.

For all that, the transplanting of agricultural lore and knowledge was as slow as the growth of the indigenous trees in the regions to the north of the Fish, the Vaal and the Tugela Rivers, where most of the black peoples farmed – the women hoeing and the men herding according to custom.

From the time when the first Free Burghers had chosen their little plots along the Liesbeek River and the Huguenots had staked out the rows of their vineyards in the mountain valleys, until the Fingoes began to buy ploughs, eight generations of farmers had settled or kept on trekking. In England the Industrial Revolution had already brought the need for more intensive farming and better implements. Before then, the farmer's plough and harrow were made by the blacksmith, his wagon by the wheelwright, and threshing machines by a local millwright with a small team of craftsmen.

Then the great agricultural implement firms began to produce – Howards of Bedford, Ransomes of Ipswich, Clayton and Shuttleworth of Lincoln, and Garrett of Leiston. Ransome discovered the chilled share and made ploughs in which the worn parts could be replaced. Howards manufactured a 'Cape plough' and in 1852 took out a patent that would revolutionise ploughing, the chilled or case-hardened mould-board share that turned the sod over. But South Africa was still predominantly pastoral. The Karoo, the Highveld and the Bushveld seemed limitless, and the pioneers were taking up huge farms they would someday divide among their sons and daughters, each receiving an equal share, but with the homestead kept for the youngest who had to care for ageing parents.

The challenge to improve output and yields from the farms only came with the economic development of the country as a whole. Not until the beginning of the 20th century was the agricultural system really called upon to make a supreme effort to satisfy the food needs of the towns. Between 1904 and 1936 the white urban population doubled itself. In 1921 there were 587 000 blacks living and working in towns; the figure had risen to 1 149 000 by 1936. Maize yields were still the second lowest in the world; cattle were plentiful, but prime beef was a luxury; the production of vegetables and sub-tropical fruits in the frost-free valleys of the Bushveld was only beginning. Farming was a way of life.

White agricultural society in South Africa had become broadly separated into two classes, the landed and the landless. Unlike Canada, America and New Zealand, there were no white farm labourers, except for the landless *bywoners* – rather like the sharecroppers in America – who did not even own oxen or implements. The base of its manpower, however, remained the blacks with the white man functioning as the skilled overseer, organising and conveying his expertise to the workers.

But more than muscle-power and sweat was required from the blacks. A typical Highveld farm, somewhere on the road between Middelburg and Bethal, where the *rooigras (Themeda triandra)* still formed a sward that looked like a field of wheat when it was in seed, well illustrates how the system worked up to the outbreak of World War I. In square thatched huts, with brightly decorated walls, there were the *woonvolk*, who lived permanently on the farms. Each of the men had acquired an individual skill which was used in an elementary system of division of labour. There was the shepherd and the herdsman, who could not count, but knew each animal and spotted at once when one was missing or sick. There was the milkman, who had been instructed in the use of a cream separator – a machine that freed the housewife from the task of skimming the milk. Then there were the drivers who could handle a long team of oxen in front of a wagon or a plough.

Planting the maize required more care and attention and this task was usually entrusted to a *bywoner*. And these landless whites were among the first to leave the land in search of more remunerative work in the towns.

The *woonvolk* did not constitute a sufficient pool of labour to meet the seasonal nature of the operations. In summer, wandering bands of Swazi walked from farm to farm to shear the sheep. The owner of the Highveld farm also had a Bushveld farm, which was nothing more than a secondary source of labour. When the first frosts fell, the Pedi who lived on it came trudging up the escarpment to reap the maize. It was a system that always tempted the owner to increase the number of blacks beyond his own labour requirements, for these squatters paid rent in cash or in kind.

All the aspects of this farming system have been investigated by numerous commissions of inquiry. It has its drawbacks and abuses, but its great advantage was that it became the main point of contact between the different cultures and an area of exchange of knowledge. Now that agriculture in South Africa has entered the new phase of conservation farming and mechanisation, the *woonvolk* are becoming the skilled, settled labour force, and the migrating seasonal labourers are remaining in the Homelands or seeking work in the towns.

In 1968 there were 4 747 000 blacks in South Africa who were classified as economically active, of whom only 683 000 worked on the 103 000 European farming units. Agriculture must face the new challenge of meeting the food demands of an exploding population, and double its output within 40 years. But experience in other countries has shown that less and not more workers will be required for the task.

Few of the products of the Homelands as yet find their way to the pantry shelves of the city housewife. But the 20 000 000 hectares of land which their inhabitants will occupy in the near future cannot only be used to meet the needs of the tillers of the soil, with a small surplus for the trading stores. The Homelands are a mere 13,7 per cent of the total area of the Republic, but they are situated for the most part within the Blue Triangle, the water-rich region of high rainfall, where good soils have a high potential productive capacity. When the present Homeland fragments are put together on a map, they form an area twice the size of Natal, the garden province of South Africa.

The old Zulu and the Xhosa chiefs would not now recognise the landscape where they looted cattle and made war. Since 1946 the soil conservation planners have been at work superimposing a new composition on Nature's faded and scarred canvas. Beginning to form are the sweeping lines of contoured grass strips, the squares of consolidated grazing areas, and the clusters of villages that grew as the widely scattered huts were brought together. The aim has not only been to protect the soil, but to increase its productivity. If the Homelands are to be viable economic units, one of the first requirements is that they should be able to feed their own growing populations.

The answer to the problem depends on the availability of land and the creation of a skilled, permanent farming class. Within those 20 000 000 hectares of land there are 35 agricultural regions. The sizes of the plots and the kind of farming will differ for each of them; and income, the crop in terms of money, will be the main factor determining how much land the farmer will have. Obviously no man will want to farm if he can earn more in the towns, the mines or the factories.

In 1955 the white agricultural experts who then had control over Homeland planning, aimed at allocating plots that would yield a gross income of R140 a year. With this as the basis of their calculations, they estimated that there would be about 357 000 little farms on which the food producers and their families would total 2 142 000 people. Using their traditional methods, these farmers would be able to produce about 4 680 000 bags of grain a year – enough for themselves and their families, but leaving no surplus for the non-farming population.

The glow of Utopian optimism in this plan was obviously fired by a gross under-estimate of the rate at which the black population was increasing. Twenty years later, when it was realised that the doubling time for the Zulu nation was only 18 years, new graphs and columns of statistics were produced to show what had to be done to meet the food demands of South Africa's total population. Scientists classifying the soil types of the Homelands calculated that, using the same methods as white farmers, they could feed at least 30 million people. The startling statement that, if South Africa was to be fed, their production would have to be increased by 1 000 per cent before the end of the century was made by a Deputy Minister in July 1977. It had by then become obvious that food, housing and employment, not ideology, were the main future problems of South Africa – and of all of Africa, for that matter.

The agriculture of the white man in South Africa has become a mighty food-producing system, the most efficient on the continent. In 1975, a good year, the total value of its products was almost two-and-a-half-billion Rand. But the country's renewable natural resources are limited. Only 15 per cent of the surface can be ploughed and of that valuable land 90 per cent is already in use, compared with but 60 per cent in Europe and America. Fresh water supplies are not abundant, and the official estimate is that there will be a shortage of about 10 per cent for domestic and industrial use by the end of this century. Since there is no more virgin land to exploit, all the emphasis is on improved methods to grow the food the big population will need within the lifetime of the next generation. So soil and water conservation have become a national aim, but the damage done by erosion in pioneering days was so great that the rate of loss is still large, possibly as much as four hundred million tonnes of topsoil a year. At present the scenario of the futurists holds political rights and geopolitical order in the full glare of the spotlight. But the actors have their feet on the ground and the way they use the good earth may decide their fate.

When Van Riebeeck planted his garden to feed mariners and merchants on their way to the wealth of the East, the population of the whole of Africa is estimated to have been only 94 million. Since then 12 generations of South African farmers have not only kept pace with the country's food needs, but are still producing a surplus for export. Now they have to face the reality of the challenge of the present population explosion: by the year 2020 there will be 70 million hungry mouths to feed – almost as many as there were in the whole of Africa when the first whites settled at the Cape. Young South Africans at school today will live in a teeming, crowded world of cities as big as present-day New York or Tokyo and off a vast veld that is cultivated like an automated factory. If they know their history, they will be grateful for the slow process that transferred the skills of the *grensboere* and the 1820 Settlers across the Fish and the Kei Rivers to the plots of the Fingoes; and for the *woonvolk* and the migratory bands of Zulu, Swazi, Pedi and Sotho that came to work and to earn money on Voortrekker farms and to learn new ways in the process. In the future mosaic of the peoples of southern Africa, the farmer will be a rare type, a man from a veld perhaps remote, but no longer unbounded.

II

The golden ladder

The ridges of rock were angled like steps where the ancient strata burst from the veld and later they were colonnaded with the skyscrapers of a new temple of wealth, the Witwatersrand. Here votaries still climb the golden ladder; and its five rungs are idols of the temple builders – the Earth Goddess that mixed gold and rock; the Randlords, captains of industry and finance; the Technicians, who found a way to break and refine the quartz-pebbled banket; the Miners, a moving concourse of black faces and the familiar white faces of the men that live and die on the property; and then the Vaal, the river of growth and decay.

The chance of finding these five factors together in one region is so remote that the ladder seems to have been assembled by Fortune herself. Without any one of the rungs this sparse farming country could never have reached the heights so soon to look into a boiling crucible of wealth and peoples – the modern metropolitan complex of the southern Transvaal.

Johannesburg grew out of the veld with the vigour of an exotic weed in fertile soil. When the prospectors discovered the reefs 92 years ago, there were few people on the Highveld and in the Bushveld of the Transvaal – about 55 000 whites, 10 000 of them English-speaking, and less than a million blacks. The old republic was then divided into 13 huge districts and the gold-bearing hills of the Witwatersrand were part of Heidelberg where there were about 300 African huts and 700 farms, an estimated total of 4 300 people.

In 1970 the population of the city of Johannesburg alone had reached 1 319 894 and the net rateable value of property had passed the R1 500 000 000 mark. On the outskirts of Alberton the last *hartbeeshuis* of a Voortrekker had been demolished ten years before, and over the hill the steel skeletons of new skyscrapers were rising above the white mine dumps.

This could never have happened if the rush, which followed the discoveries of the prospectors – Fred and Harry Struben, J. G. Bantjes, George Walker and George Harrison – had been the mere ebb and flow of a tide of fortune hunters. And at first there was an air of uncertainty and impermanence about the future of the new fields. Indeed, the owner of the farm where Harrison had discovered the Main Reef, after scribbling a hasty note to President Kruger, set off as usual that year to the winter grazing of the Bushveld. Rumours of gold still meant so little to the routine of Voortrekker life.

Previous experience in California and in Australia had given the first miners no means of judging the value of the new field. In the formation of these conglomerates the Earth Goddess had created a unique treasure. The main tool she used was undoubtedly the water of a great lake, but it is now thought that untold trillions of bacteria and lichens, the oldest form of life known to man, may have helped her with the work. The rock which the miners found in the oxidized 'free milling' zone of the outcrop looked like the almond sweetmeat for which the Dutch name is 'banket'. It consists mainly of white and smoky quartz pebbles bound together in a siliceous cement.

Man sought only the gold that was rarely visible to the naked eye, but Nature seems to have scraped the earth to make a mixture that contains sections of cubes and pentagonal dodecahedra and octahedra of pyrites, 'fools' gold', chlorite, sericite, zircon, pink grains of corrundum and tourmaline needles – even greenish diamonds. The geology, mineralogy, chemistry and physics of the Witwatersrand, down to a depth of 3 600 metres, have been studied more intensively than any other slice of the earth's great crust. The uranium that was found may, as the Atomic Age marches on, become a source of power more valuable than the gold that is guarded in vaults. Down in the depths even the tracks of meson particles are being followed as science advances along the road to understanding anti-matter.

But the problems of the gold miners were very material indeed. The reefs dipped down at an angle and posed two questions: would they continue to yield gold all the way and how deep could man go to loot the hoard? An American mining paper warned, 'Even Methuselah died'. Among the tents and hovels of Ferreira's Camp the pessimists began to pack up and the optimists threw empty bottles at them. But six years after the discovery, a small diamond drill intersected the reef at a depth of 721 metres. The core, less than three centimetres in diameter, contained payable gold. Since then, although there are rich and poor areas, deep-level mining has proved that the gold-content is remarkably consistent in these conglomerates. Many mines could be opened, based merely on borehole results from which experts calculate ore reserves, working costs and the profits which invested capital might expect. If it were not for this geological freak, which made it possible to predict values down to more than 4 000 metres, the gold mines of the Witwatersrand would never have been more than the world's biggest gamble – a lucky dip that cost millions to put a shovel into.

In July 1886 Fred Alexander, a produce merchant, took samples of the banket from the Rand to the diamond mines at Kimberley and exhibited them in his store. When they were crushed and panned, the diamond magnates at once sniffed gold in the air – and from that day they were on the road to becoming Randlords.

Kimberley had been their kindergarten of mining and high finance. With the caution and cunning of their kind, they began to estimate the value of the find. Barney Barnato, deterred by an expert report, bided his time. Cecil Rhodes ignored the experts, bought claims and began to raise capital in England with the message, 'The Rand is the biggest thing the world has seen'. He was no novice at the game of company promotion. J. B. Robinson bought portions of the farms Turffontein and Langlaagte for R52 000. The diggers laughed and called this virgin veld 'Robinson's cabbage patch'. But soon these properties were valued at R36 000 000 and within five years they had paid R2 000 000 in dividends to shareholders.

The second rung of the golden ladder, the Randlords, was placed in position by young men who were still in their thirties and worked hard and bargained hard as they consolidated the claims and smaller companies. The mines were so big and costly that they could never have been a one-man show.

One of South Africa's most eminent historians, Professor C. W. de Kiewiet, in 1941 summed up the achievement of the Randlords in these terms: 'the gold mines were a spectacular demonstration of how far a capitalistic industry working for profit could go to increase efficiency of management and operation.' Only in the political field, in warmongering and intrigue, did these men leave a black record that has almost overshadowed their financial achievements.

But all the problems of the mines would not be settled in a haze of cigar smoke in boardrooms and clubs. There had to be men at work in the laboratories as well. At first the oxidised ores near the surface had been crushed in stamp batteries and the gold recovered on amalgam plates, a mixture of metal and mercury. At depth the banket turned bluish and glittered with pyrites, the 'fools' gold', that ate up the mercury.

The crisis was so serious that Cecil Rhodes is reported to have sold all his shares. It was solved by the application of the cyanide process, discovered in Glasgow in 1887 by John Stuart MacArthur and the brothers Forrest. An experimental plant, set up at the Robinson Mine in November 1890, treated 10 000 tonnes of tailings. The minute grains of gold then began to enter a new phase of their immortal lives in a manner very similar to the childhood they spent, hundreds of millions of years ago, among the silt particles of the great lake. The hills of the Witwatersrand reverberated with the mechanical thunder of stamp batteries that pulverised the banket down to the fine grains of the original mother rock. The pulp then settled in the agitated waters or precipitating tanks and after that the sand was subjected to cyanide treatment, where the beautiful metal surrendered itself to the deadly poison. Within three years 18 tonnes of gold, then valued at R3 545 000, had come out of the process in a 12-month period.

But the Technicians, the third rung of the ladder, had to evolve the efficiency of the mass-production assembly line in this gigantic underground quarry before the few ounces of gold in each cubic yard of rock could be mined at a profit. Dynamite factories, pneumatic drills to make holes for the charges, tube mills to take the place of stamp batteries, conveyor belts, air purification to keep the deadly silicon dust out of human lungs, refrigeration plants to cool deep subterranean passages, and powerful electric hoists to lower men and raise ore in vertical drops of more than 1,6 kilometres – all became components of the huge manufacturing plant that began at the rock-face and ended with the pouring of the gold bars in the refinery.

It was a single industry with all the elements of an industrial revolution; and it was a training ground that gave its workers the mental outlook and many of the skills that would be required in factories producing consumer goods in all the variety that is needed to satisfy the present-day demands of southern Africa and its neighbours.

But the horny hands and sweat of toil were needed in the dark depths as much as machines. The fourth rung of the ladder, the Workers, was often obscenely articulate. Shouts and oaths were like vocal balm in that hellish workplace; and they echoed down the drives, along the haulages and into the stopes above the hissing of pistons, the muttering of gears and the whine of electric motors. The stopes, the keyholes to the treasure chest, are mere slits in the rock that follow the angle of dip of the reefs. Their roofs are low to prevent the mining of waste rock; the worker crawls into them with his drill, and they are one of the main reasons why it is not possible to mine with powerful rockcutting tools. Nature herself has determined that human hands must perform a multiplicity of tasks to get at the thin bands of banket in which the particles of gold are embedded.

The job soon evolved into an almost traditional system of division of labour. A white miner supervised the drilling operations of the blacks, who kicked and shoved at the pneumatic jackhammers; he marked the holes and gave the direction the drill had to take; then he charged up with dynamite and supervised the firing. Every stoper had his gang and in addition to the operators of the drills there were often also drill-carriers, handlers of the pneumatic picks, lashers – the word is derived from the Xhosa *laisha,* to load – who moved the broken rock with a shovel, and a 'piccanin', now a herder of rocks, to light up the fuses and run errands. Some of the workers, the contractors, were on piece-work and others were on day's pay – and skilled white pay was so good that miners were attracted from all over the world down into the depths below the sunny hills of the Witwatersrand. And from the rural areas of South Africa and neighbouring states came black contract workers who risked rockbursts, heat exhaustion and the long lonely separation from their families when they signed up for their stints on the mines. It is hard and dangerous work, until recently poorly paid, but it achieved a certain mystique of its own, for the men who go underground are the heroes of the workforce and for many young men it has replaced the rigours of the initiation school as proof of adulthood.

The familiar term 'reef' itself was a reminder of sailors who had taken part in the gold rush to Ballarat and Bendigo in Australia. To them any rock sticking out above the surface was a reef, no matter whether it was in the sea or on land. But as the Rand grew, the mining Moloch devoured an endless procession of sacrificial labour. It craved muscled, skilled men most of all.

The pick of these toilers in the earth's depths came from Cornwall and the Scilly Isles, where Carthaginians had fetched their tin as long ago as the 2nd century B.C. They came just as eagerly from Lancashire, Yorkshire and Northumberland. There came, too, the Welshmen, whose ancestors had mined coal for Trevithick's first steam-engine, and they were adept at timbering the shafts.

Johannesburg, like New York, which Bryce called 'a European city but of no particular country', became a melting-pot of languages, accents and cultures; and from this brew there emerged first of all 'the miners', then 'the Jo'burgites', and finally, in a generation or two, 'the South Africans', most of whom spoke the two languages of the country, English and Afrikaans. The process continued as immigrants, a quarter of a million in five years, streamed in from many European countries, from Yugoslavia in the east all the way to Ireland.

Their destination is no longer only the mines, but the whole spectrum of industry which is developing in the process of a vital economic upsurge. New genes, older traditions, different values, strange customs and foods and, above all, varied ways of interpreting the world around them – the *dorps* and cities, the veld and bush – arrive with every batch of these future South Africans. Each of them contributes something unique to the life of the country, like a new thread in a tapestry or another tile in the mosaic. But all of them retain links of memory and blood with the mother countries – the *stamlande*, as the Afrikaners call them.

The Afrikaners themselves were being affected to an increasing extent by this process since the arrival of the Dutch in 1652 and the French Huguenots in 1688. In September 1977 Professor Johan Degenaar of Stellenbosch University gave the result of demographic research which showed that the Afrikaner nation is now composed of the following elements: 34,8 per cent German; 33,7 per cent Dutch; 13,2 per cent French; 6,9 per cent non-whites; 5,2 per cent British; 2,7 per cent other European nations; 3,5 per cent unknown.

The mines also attracted a constant stream of blacks. At first they walked, often following footpaths that had been trodden when they migrated down Africa, to get from the kraals to the compounds, their new living quarters, which were named after the Malay *kampong*, the enclosure in which a house or factory stood. And the blacks came to sell their labour, not to settle. At the end of their contracts they had to return to their families and the graves of their ancestors – they were not to be men of the city. In the compounds, bachelor quarters became home for men lonely for their families far away. For the women, the aged and the children left behind on the land there was the instability of family life without fathers and able-bodied men.

In 1899 there were about 110 000 men in the compounds and they vanished back into the bush while the white men fought their war for three years. The graphs of output and dividends closely followed that of the total labour force, but South Africa itself never seemed to have enough blacks prepared to satisfy the demand. In 1904 the mines were permitted to bring in 50 000 Chinese coolies, mainly from Hong Kong, and this began a furore that had far-reaching political effects. In the Transvaal the politicians and the white miners talked of the 'Chinese peril'; in England the cry was Chinese slavery, and when the Balfour ministry fell a Liberal Government was elected in its place. It set South Africa on the road to independence and the ultimate creation of the Republic of South Africa.

In time the black labour force of all the mines was almost 400 000 and the output of gold was more than 800 tonnes a year. In the compounds there were now men who could tell tales of the cattle country in Mozambique along the lower reaches of the Limpopo; of the fishing in Lake Malawi; of the pouring rains in the Angola highlands; of the coming of the floods in Barotseland, when the King's barges made their ceremonial journey down the river; of the adventure of the trek to the mines – their first train journey, the crossing of the wide Zambesi River in a small launch, or of a flight across the great thorn-desert expanses of the Kalahari.

This was also one of the most important crossings of psychological, language, cultural and economic borders in all southern Africa. It was the meeting-place of Europe's Industrial Revolution with the Iron Age of Africa – of the hoe with the pneumatic drill, of the team of oxen with the steam-engine and the electric motor, of the hospital and the syringe with the *muti* of the diviner.

On a scale far greater than the native trader's store, the gold mines also created new demands. When the workers returned, they were the heroes of foreign travel in the villages. The old men gathered round the beer pots to hear about *iGoli*, the city of gold. Many of the maidens would not marry a man who had not made that romantic journey to *iGoli* to come back with a coffer filled with goods bought at the concession store. The herdboys gaped and dreamed of becoming miners someday.

Yet, the system has been pounded with criticism from all sides. Trade unionists, syndicalists, socialists, communists and well-meaning reformers all threw arguments like stones at the compounds. There had been from the start a horizontal border of skills in the mines, which sharply separated the white and the black workers. The whites feared an invasion of their territory and they protected an industrial heartland, what they saw as the 'civilised standard'. Even the rule of the rate for the job proved an inadequate weapon and a system of job reservation was introduced. But all the reformers wanted the very opposite – the breakdown of that horizontal border, the colour bar. The war is still raging, and there appears to be no hope of an early peace. But the white flag of truce is being raised in other industries, where the border is not so sharply defined and skills migrate with the movement of the production line.

Of all those who helped to build the Rand the black miners contributed one of the largest shares; and the Rand gave them something of value in return: the concept (or is it a tyranny?) of time in the timeless world of Africa; the hoot of the sirens that ordered the shifts; the meaning of output in relation to earnings; the buying power of money and the creativeness of team work and management in an industrial process. All these were new ideas in southern Africa which needs them to build its factories and produce food for its future millions.

The fifth rung of the ladder, the Vaal River, is 50 kilometres to the south of the line along which the Reef outcropped between the hills, where the Voortrekkers found the white water of streamlets sparkling down the slopes into the *pans* (water holes). At first these streams slaked by the bucketful the thirst of the mining camp. But when they dried up during droughts, water could not be had for love or money – and there was always plenty of both in Johannesburg.

Those were the days when crisis was the best planner, because nobody looked very far ahead. As the tents and shacks took on the permanence of a town, as the Randlords began to erect prefabricated houses and mansions above Doornfontein's springs, as the compounds grew bigger and more stamp batteries thundered, boreholes were sunk into the underground water of the dolomite caverns. As the taps were turned on, every new scheme was hailed as a permanent solution. But Johannesburg, as it still does, continued to grow faster than its water supplies.

Engineering forecasts, like false prophecies, were belied when another crisis followed the promise of abundance. In desperation the golden octopus sent out the tentacles of pipelines to a barrage on the Vaal River. When that proved inadequate, the concrete wall of a big dam was built – and raised and raised. Today the Rand is augmenting its supply from the Tugela River by pumping water up the eastern slopes of the Drakensberg. Blueprints are ready for water to flow all the way from Botswana's Okavango Delta, where luxuriant wildlife now teems in the swamps, to supply not only the city of the gold mines but its unborn sibling, the great mining venture which will be undertaken in the Bushveld Igneous Complex to the north of the old metropolis.

A good indicator of the living standard of a people is the amount of water they use. For the blacks it may mark the transition from carrying a clay pot on the head to a tap in the kitchen. On the Rand the daily consumption of water has grown over the past 26 years from 160 litres to 360 litres per capita. It has been a great civil engineering feat to pump and reticulate about 1 300 000 tonnes of water a day and to plan ahead for future needs which the Rand Water Board estimates will double every 12 years.

The great Pretoria-Witwatersrand-Vereeniging metropolitan region has become the mechanical suction pump of South Africa's natural heartland. It draws in people but does not circulate them back to the villages and kraals. Myth as well as the realities of the labour market attract them to an area producing almost two-thirds of the nation's yearly income. Even so the pump cannot cope with the flood.

In 1973 it was estimated that 70 000 black workers come onto the labour market every year, as compared with only 8 000 who can find work in the Homelands. The annual cost of creating job opportunities for them was about R445 million, 2,5 per cent of the country's gross domestic product. So the alternative plan to the Greater Rand is the creation out of the foundation of dorps and veld of 24 new cities in South Africa by the year 2 000 A.D. Within a generation there will be 22 000 000 blacks in the boiling-pot of acculturation – city life. So the key sociopsychological question remains: How much of their language and traditions will they bring with them? How many of the ancestral spirits need migrate from the cattle kraals to the townships with their orthodox churches and new religious sects, with their shebeens (the speakeasies of black South Africa), and with schools that may burn like funeral pyres as the inexorable process moves on.

Compared with the Nile, the muddy river that drains the veld is a mere trickle; and so Hottentot, black and Boer described it in turn as the *kyGarieb*, the *iLikwa* and the Vaal. But it has built its own pyramids, the grey mounds of the mine dumps, and concrete towers are its minarets from which the faithful are called to worship according to the creed of Hollard Street, where the stock exchange receives them.

Without the Vaal River the wealth of the Witwatersrand could never have been fully exploited. The steps that were taken to satisfy the Rand's water needs were another training ground that was to benefit the whole of South Africa. Here engineers and hydrologists for the first time learned to plan and control a multi-purpose river system, which included not only the Rand but the big irrigation scheme at Vaalharts. It became a prototype which could be copied wherever other rivers were put to work to satisfy the needs of a growing population. In a country where water supplies are the main limiting factor to future development, this fifth rung of the golden ladder may yet prove to be the most valuable aid of all in the upward climb of the peoples of southern Africa.

12

The neotechnic age

Iron Age people in southern Africa had their primitive ISCOR (Iron and Steel Corporation). Fragments of it have been unearthed by archaeologists at Uitkomst, one of the numerous smelting sites between the Magaliesberg and the Witwatersrand. From these remains a ground plan can be drawn of the factories that puffed the smoke of thorn tree logs and charcoal a thousand years ago.

A clay smelting furnace, covered with a conical pot, held only a couple of kilograms of iron ore at a time. On either side of it there were earthen platforms for bellows that could be worked simultaneously. Their blasts were directed into the melting chamber by two clay *tuyeres*, the furnace nozzles. Flat stone slabs, worn from the pounding, show where weathered ore from the surface lodes was crushed.

From this slow process of smelting the people had to make the basic equipment for their agriculture, warfare and hunting – spear blades stuck into wooden shafts, hafted adzes, hoes with tangs and the mining tool, a kind of combined crowbar and chisel. This culture was part of an immense development that grew and spread in Africa south of the Sahara for many centuries. The prehistoric outlines have been redrawn by modern research and they reveal remarkable ingenuity. It is puzzling that the blacks, who inherited much from this older culture, never took it further along the road of technical achievement.

Many of the white pioneers actually saw the black ironsmiths at work. The basic technique differed only slightly from tribe to tribe. The assegais with which the Zulu *impis* attacked the Voortrekkers were mostly the products of a clan that lived in the Pietermaritzburg district. All the men, young and old, had been trained to do this work. In other tribes the secrets of the ironsmith were passed on from father to sons. The special rites, the doctoring of the ore with *muti*, gave an air of mystery to the pounding of the bellows and the smoke of the furnaces.

But these furnaces were not destined to be the womb of the

future industrialisation of the blacks. The fertilized seeds spread to the Cape from Europe in ships that were one of the finest products of the eotechnic phase – the age when the watermills were supplying most of the motive power for the sawmills and grindstones. But a country in the pioneer agricultural stage of development was not much of an overseas market. In 1870 the white population, spread from Table Bay to the wagon drifts on the Limpopo River, was only 317 000.

By then Europe was well into the paleotechnic phase of machine industry – the great coal-and-iron complex. South Africa had got no further than the use of skilled hands to guide the tools that were needed to build houses and make furniture and wagons. Much of the work was done by Malay and coloured craftsmen. The Malays brought with them an expert knowledge of wood carving and many of the period pieces of stinkwood furniture, still in use in South African homes, are monuments to their skill. They left, too, a lasting mark of Holland's links with the East – the hallmark of a good stinkwood piece, claw-and-ball feet, which symbolize the Oriental legend of the pearl of beauty gripped in the talons of the beast.

In the eastern border country of the *hartbeeshuis* and the more impressive Cape-Dutch homes of officialdom at Graaff-Reinet, the blacks fetched and carried, shoved and lifted, but handled no tools. It was the craftsmen, not the master builders, that drew the horizontal line of the barrier of skills. Above it was the territory which they have guarded jealously right up to the present time. Again, it was the missionaries who attempted to fully integrate the blacks into this system – timid pioneers in a land proliferating the new weapons with which man was attempting to control and change his natural environment.

The Cape *White Book* of 1849 has left a brief description of the workshops at 32 mission institutions where blacks were being trained. There were still very few of them. Out of a total of 2 713 adult males at the missions there were seven thatchers, 21 carpenters, five basket makers, one blacksmith, six hut makers, one brick-maker and 15 wagon makers. The carpenter's bench was a new wonderland, for most of them had never seen a screw or a nail, a vice, a plane, the battery of chisels, or the trowel and measuring instruments of the builders – the rule, the T-square, the spirit level, the compass and the mason's plumb-line. They had not learned how to draw a circle and the round grass huts of the villages were of all shapes and sizes.

Long ago Europe had experienced the intense mediaevel activity of cathedral building and clock-making. But the greatest architectural achievement of the Zulu nation was the construction of the king's hut with its beaded pillars and polished mud-and-dung floor.

Technical invention alone, whether in Europe or America, did not determine the pace of the coming of the Machine Age. There had to be cultural preparation – a change of mind, new desires, habits, ideas and goals. As its population grew and became an economic market, South Africa could have made a rapid transition by importing machines from more advanced countries. But the people, the white farmers and the black herdsmen, had to be made ready for them; and it was in this respect that the mines played such an important part in stimulating secondary industry.

An analysis of what the mines spent in 1947 indicates the extent to which they had become the customer of industries that had been stimulated by the restrictions which two world wars had imposed on the exchange of goods with overseas countries. Some R16 million was paid for local metal goods such as steel cables, piping and tubing, rock drills, pumps, rails, electric cables and wires. The R9 million which went to the chemical industry was not only for explosives but also for chemicals, carbide, paints, oils and greases. The hides from the farmers' herds and some of the wool from their sheep was included in the R3 million paid for clothing and footwear. Great forests of pines and blue gums, the seeds of which had been brought in from Mexico, the British Honduras and Australia, had been planted on the mountain slopes of the Eastern Transvaal mist belt, and R5 million worth of timber was brought in to prop the tunnels underground. Big coal-burning power stations supplied electricity worth R10 million a year for light and energy. Within four years, as the industrial boom began to gather momentum, the shift from the overseas to the local industrial market was still more obvious. By 1970 mines were spending R52 million on South African and R13 million on imported goods.

The treasure chest, filled with bars of gold, at first made South Africans forget that the chest was made of iron. But the growing needs of the metal industries forced the young state, the Union of South Africa, to turn its eyes to another treasure – Thabazimbi, the mountain of iron. Once again the expertise to exploit this wealth had to come from countries that were already well into the neotechnic phase of industrial development, the electricity-and-alloy complex. German experts in 1928 advised the building of a steelworks near Pretoria, in the same broad valley where the Iron Age smiths had stoked their clay furnaces.

But South Africa's cultural and educational development was such that it was already producing experts of its own – men who would be able to design a second and third steelworks and decide where to erect them. The pioneering giant among these indigenous experts was Dr H. J. van der Bijl, who guided the development of ISCOR, the first works, and also became the chairman of the Electricity Supply Commision (ESCOM). These enterprises depended at first on government finance and General Smuts was one of the critics who maintained that they were the needless desire of economic nationalism for self-sufficiency. But he changed his mind; and when he opened the headquarters of ESCOM, Johannesburg's first skyscraper, he spoke proudly of 'state capitalism'.

The country now had not only raw materials but a source of energy and in 1945 General Smuts himself set up the Council for Scientific and Industrial Research. Sir Basil Schonland, the eminent physicist, was its first director, and his task was to apply to industry the scientific methods that were an essential element of the neotechnic phase, and distinguished it from the previous age when it was mainly practical men who produced the steam-engine, the railways, the textile mill and the iron ship in England.

Both above and below the horizontal border of skills, industry began to absorb workers voraciously. A total labour force of 120 900 in 1926 grew to 379 000 in 1946. By 1968 the economically active workers in private industry included 1 289 528 blacks, 374 490 whites, 209 211 coloureds and 65 932 Asians. The country as a whole was producing more goods and services, and the national income rose from R750 million in 1929 to R21 250 million in 1974. In terms of welfare this meant that the real income per head increased from R82 to R174 a year during the same period. The country could boast that the standard of living of its many millions of people was already from five to 12 times higher than that of any country in the Afro-Asian world.

Among the mine dumps the saw-toothed roofs of factories not only sheltered batteries of new machines from Europe and America, but also Zulu, Sotho, Pondo, Ndebele and Pedi workers, who had been drawn from their villages by the magnet of *iGoli*. But they did not come to mine gold. They were outside of the system which transported married men to the Rand, housed and fed them in compounds, and sent them back at the end of each contract period.

In the factories, where a greater degree of skill demanded continuity of service, there could not be a rapid rate of labour turnover if the embryonic systems of mass production were to function efficiently. So the blacks brought their families with them to this Eldorado of steel, arising on the surface above the underground rattle of the jackhammer drills.

In the Homelands the little plots were becoming smaller and poorer; and so they came to stay – faster than houses could be built for them. And there were those who said: 'Let them stay!' Like the ghosts of Manchester economists, they talked about labour markets and the worker's right to freedom of movement as he sought the highest price for his services. It was the Utopianism of *laissez-faire* in a world of planned and controlled development. But economic freedom, like justice, is often victim of other pressures such as population growth, the balancing of urban and rural environments, and planned re-settlement to achieve a state of equilibrium in a given *milieu*.

The imbalance of birth-rate and death-rate had given warning of its coming in South Africa. In 36 years after the outbreak of World War II the population increased from 10 170 000 to 25 471 000. In Johannesburg the black population grew from 118 652 in 1921 to 650 912 in 1960. The Department of Statistics estimates that South Africa's whites will double by the year 2010 and by 2012 the coloureds and blacks will treble their 1970 levels. The whites will then be 8,7 million, the coloureds 7,3 million and the blacks 54,6 million.

These developments, the new factories and the new babies, brought something dark and desperate, as well as great wealth, to Johannesburg. Industrialisation was following the old path, trodden so wearily by the Industrial Revolution in England. The first atomic bomb had not yet been dropped when the city mushroomed, round the central pillar of its commercial area, with the smoke of thousands of braziers in the shanty-towns. Once again, the influx of workers was greater than the need. Forsaking tribal life and discipline in their kraals of grass huts, the black men came to those architectural scarecrows, the shanties, put together with flattened tins and old sacks.

These areas of urban squalor were held aloft like ragged banners for all the world, especially the United Nations, to see how bad South Africa was. But Johannesburg was merely going through an experience similar to that of Greater Calcutta, where a population of three million at the time of the partition of India in 1947 had increased to 12 million by 1969. Drought drove the peasants of Bihar from their smallholdings to Calcutta, and the tide was swelled by refugees from East Pakistan. In Johannesburg the new arrivals built their shanties; in Calcutta those that did not sleep on the city pavements in their *dhoties* built huts of reeds or palm leaves in colonies known as *bustees*. Calcutta's plan of salvation had three major objectives: regional and city planning, urban renewal and the establishment of three other major cities elsewhere in West Bengal. Johannesburg followed a similar road, but the policy of segregation complicated and slowed the process – social and political motivation did not necessarily follow the same paths.

The South African Government began by passing legislation to control the influx. It cleared the shanty-towns and then, using teams of specially trained black artisans, it built 75 540 houses in Johannesburg by 1966. The new townships were planned with community centres, recreation facilities, hospitals, shops and a primary school for every 800 families. Regional plans were prepared for the Republic as a whole, providing for decentralisation and the establishment of 24 new nodes of development – the cities of the future. The Tugela River Basin, with its great water wealth, was planned like a precisely cut gem. In 1972 a third ISCOR began production at Newcastle and sparked off the formation of a new metropolitan complex that will ultimately provide work and housing for 20 million people. The old battlefields of Voortrekkers and Zulus, of Boer and Briton, will be overlaid by highways, green-belt recreation areas, and the apartments of high-density living.

The soil of the Homelands cannot give a living to more people and so steps have to be taken to house and employ at least 23 million blacks in urban areas within the next 30 years. It is a stupendous task for a small country, but the planners, if not the mass of the population, are aware of this. In the Homelands themselves 84 new towns are being built and another 36 are on the drawing-boards. The big new nodes of development are being sited in border areas, so that they will be able to absorb black workers, while keeping true to the policy of the ethnic heartlands.

In South Africa, apart from the warnings of small voluntary associations of conservationists, like the National Veld Trust, there have been few Club-of-Rome pessimists to define the rapidly approaching limits of growth – especially those imposed by available arable land and water supplies. The country's mineral wealth, still regarded as inexhaustible, is the lodestar of planners who want South Africa to develop as the industrial giant of the continent.

The course has been set by the Prime Minister's Economic Advisory Council: an annual 6,4 per cent economic growth rate to make jobs for the 75 000 to 95 000 blacks coming into the labour market every year.

Black youngsters in the Transkei or KwaZulu acquire the skills of their society – making toy clay oxen and wagons, a rawhide whip, traps for birds while they learn the adjectives that describe the colours of 80 different types of cattle. But an electric switch and a water tap are innovations to many of them. Dr A. T. Bryant has described the working of a Zulu smithy and the making of *inTshimbi*, iron implements that included assegais *(umKonto)*, hoes *(iLembe)*, axes *(iZembe)*, awls *(uSungulo)*, and knives *(umuKwa)*. But these were families of hereditary craftsmen, not a production line.

The industrial school has taken the place of the carpenter's bench at the mission station. During 1975, schemes for the in-service training of black factory operators in white industrial complexes were of benefit to 55 591 of these workers. But most experts are agreed that a critical shortage of skilled labour is the main bottleneck hindering industrial expansion. One answer is to supplement it by some 62 000 immigrants every year.

Meanwhile the tribal midwives wash newborn babies with infusions of *uMalali* herbs; and in the maternity wards of new township hospitals there are no vacant beds. The greatest wish, the proudest joy, of every black woman is being fulfilled while the family planners look on in dismay. The result is that the yearly growth rate of the black population is 2,9 per cent, whereas that of the whites is but 1,2 per cent. When this baby boom has passed through the schools, it will join the historic 'trek to look for work'.

The doors have not always been wide open to receive it. The legal system gives the skilled labour force a layered structure by defining the tasks the different races may undertake in the mines and industries. It is only in their own Homelands that blacks can rise to all levels of responsibility. There are barriers in the white areas, but due to the shortage of labour so many exemptions are granted that the reality belies the lawbook ideal. A commission which is busy examining the South African labour laws has found that their repeal would not go to the heart of the problem – the relationship of black and white workers to each other at the work-bench. The territorial borders of the land of skilled work have all but vanished from the economic map, but not from the hearts of the individual workers.

In spite of the cultural difficulties the growth of South African industry has been one of the success stories of a land that was veld and bush when James Watt constructed his steam-engine in 1765. In 1970 the industrial census distinguished 19 groups in the manufacturing sector. They had some 13 200 establishments producing a gross output of R7 503 million, and materials used in the production of this output were valued at R4 415 million, giving a net output of R3 088 million. During the census year the salaries and wages of a working force of 1 091 000 in that sector amounted to R1 414 million.

These new industries, whether in the Homelands, on their borders or around the white urban areas, are weaving new threads of human relationship in the tapestry of a plural society. The black herdsmen and the women that worked with hoes in the fields have proved that they adapt rapidly to the factory environment and become proficient 'herders of machines'.

In their minds there is curiosity about the designing, the making, the assembling and the maintenance of a modern economy and many have all but forgotten the craftsman who doctored his forge with medicines. Where the clay furnaces smoked, there is not only the steelworks of Pretoria but the atomic pile at Pelindaba. And when they dream, as they perform the repetitive tasks of mass production, it is of their children becoming engineers and scientists. No man that loves South Africa and her peoples will deny them the dreams that are becoming conscious ambitions and then, hopefully, realities.

I

1. *This sea, in gracious mood, belies the fear it struck in early mariners who rounded Cape Point on their journeys to the East. Past this rocky promontory, the vessels of today face the same monstrous seas and angry storms that destroyed the ships of another era, and even now cast wrecks upon the shore.*

2. *Beyond the cold Atlantic waters of the bay, the sandstone cliffs of Table Mountain stand at the masthead of Africa. Of old, the hinterland held myth and death – the treasures of Monomotapa, deserts, arid Karoo, tall forest, sweet grassveld and thorn-bush wherein to seek a crop of ivory. The first wheel tracks that left the Fort of Good Hope to cross the Liesbeek River and head for the distant mountains have become modern highways that link a mosaic of peoples and wealth from Agulhas to Capricorn. Along them traffic flows through the heart of a vast land that was beating with life before trade followed the flag or a forge and anvil had been unloaded from the blacksmith's wagon.*

3   4

3. *Cape Town is a city where people can watch the world go by. The Witwatersrand produces almost two-thirds of the country's wealth, yet it has to endure the jibe that once a man has made his fortune among the mine dumps, he comes to the Mother City to enjoy it. But it would be wrong to assume that Cape Town has been lulled into complacency by her historical importance. The streets are filled with commercial bustle and the harbour, newly extended for the age of containerisation, is evidence of her broader interests. Although she ranks behind Durban as a port and Johannesburg as an industrial centre, in many spheres of endeavour she has maintained supremacy; the garment industry, shipbuilding and engineering, fish and food processing are all large and successful ventures. Yet for the thousands of tourists who visit each year, it is her unique natural setting that assures her vaunted position among the cities of the world.*

4. *The Indian and Atlantic Oceans, levers of geo-political power, have as their symbolic fulcrum the mountainous Cape Peninsula, seen here from the air. Once an island, it is now joined to the African main-land (left of the photograph) by sandy flats, the first obstacle the white man faced as he migrated inland. Its gentle Mediterranean climate helped make this small region the most successful settlement of Europeans on the Dark Continent three centuries ago.*

5

5. *Man of vision of an earlier age, Jan van Riebeeck, company servant and administrator extraordinary, looks out over the city he founded. But had he stood at this actual spot the tide would have ebbed at his feet. A bold land reclamation scheme begun after the First World War extended the foreshore area and glass and steel monoliths now crowd where the trading fleets of the Age of Navigation once lay at anchor.*

6. *Cape Town's heart, a cluster of tall concrete buildings, stands where sailors once rolled water barrels down Jan van Riebeeck's wooden jetty to the fleets of Indiamen carrying spices to Europe. Where some 90 men came in 1652 to build a refreshment station for passing ships, a million people live today.*

7. *In Table Bay yachts rigged for racing often fleck the blue water between supertankers. In the 325 years since Van Riebeeck sailed his three small vessels into the bay, Cape Town has played host to the world.*

8

9

8. *Back in geological time, before wind and water eroded it down, Table Mountain was five times as high as it is today. The daring Portuguese navigator Antonio de Saldanha climbed up Platteklip Gorge to reach the top in 1503; but, while its various routes still challenge South Africa's youth, a cable-car permits an easy ascent today.*

9. *The mountains dip their feet in the waves along the wild and beautiful shoreline that stretches from the city to Cape Point. The intertidal zone was once the territory of Strandlopers who, though related to the nomad Hottentots (Xhoi), owned no cattle and subsisted on shellfish, mussels and roots. Like the Hottentots, they lost their identity through intermarriage with foreigners and their lives through smallpox brought from across the sea.*

10–15. The chill waters of Cape Town's Costa del Sol invite sunbathing on tiny coves nestling among tumbled boulders. But the city has two coasts and the warm waters of False Bay attract many to its broad white beaches.

16

18

17

16. *Two coloured children, young buds on a family tree with deep roots in the soil of three continents. The 2,3 million people of mixed blood, designated 'coloured' in South Africa, are truly indigenous, for their history begins in Africa where their bloodlines met and mingled after the first European stepped ashore at the Cape. White colonists and mariners added their genes to those of the Hottentot and Bushmen. Soon new elements were added to the infusion –*

Malay, African, Indian, Chinese, European. The coloureds share the same values as the whites, speak the same languages (for the most part Afrikaans), and belong to the same churches. Many, if not the majority belong to the working-class and excel as artisans and industrial and farm workers. But more and more are taking white-collar jobs, and recent years have seen the rise of an influential coloured middle-class.

17. Lunch hour in the sun beside the historic Grand Parade, once the scene of military parades, dramatic official announcements and the loud oratory of reform. Rapid city growth has made it a parking lot and sometime flea market.

18. This avenue of oaks began as a broadwalk beside the Company Gardens where the Dutch tilled the soil and grew fruit and vegetables for passing ships. Now a beautiful breathing-space in the heart of the city, these gardens recall the labours and purpose of the early founders who brought from the cultivated fields of Europe the agrarian tradition still deeply ingrained in the South African way of life.

19   20
21   22

19–22. The genetic links with Asia, Africa and Europe are evident in these faces.

23. The fish vendor's seaweed horn is heard no longer, but a few horse-drawn carts still ply Cape Town's streets selling products of sea and soil.

24

25

24. *District Six, the former heartland of the coloured people, is now all but demolished and its inhabitants resettled in new housing estates on the city outskirts. Yet far more than bricks and mortar have been lost beneath the bulldozers' treads: with every wall that fell went the humour, lifestyle and dialect of a unique community.*

25. The Malay Quarter on the steep slopes of Signal Hill is an architectural vestige where freed slaves, many of them skilled craftsmen, once built small houses that incorporated elements of Cape Dutch and Georgian styles they saw in the houses of their masters: high stoeps with steps on either side, attractive cornices, fanlights and windows with small panes. The walls are of various tints and at intervals slender minarets of mosques break the straight lines. Here the Malays lived as a group that retained its social and religious identity, fortified by Islam. The struggle to preserve the Quarter has led to the creation of a restoration plan. The photograph contrasts slum conditions with the achievements of renewal work.

26

27

26. *Flowers and silk spreads in the tomb of a Muslim holy man* (Tuan) *where the faithful come to pray and meditate. Round Cape Town the tombs of the* Tuans *form a mystic circle believed to protect the followers of Mohammed from natural disasters. One of these remarkable men, Tuan Guru, transcribed the Koran from memory in the mid-18th century when there was no copy available at the Cape. But this feat of memory is in many ways eclipsed by the power of faith among the Cape Malays who, without the written word to guide them and cut off from the mainstream of orthodox Islam in the Middle East, clung to the tenets of the faith they brought with them as slaves and exiles from the East Indies in the early days of the settlement.*

27. *A leader of Cape Town's Muslim community, Sheikh Suleiman Mosaval, gives counsel both secular and religious. Islam is a powerful force among its adherents who, although they constitute a mere 6,4% of the whole, make up an influential sector of the coloured population.*

28. Within hearing of the Muezzin's *call there is the hypnotic beat of tom-toms – the* rabannas *– used at a Cape Malay* Khalifa. *Science cannot explain why the votaries do not bleed as they cut and hack themselves with swords and daggers and pierce their skins with skewers. It may be no more than skilful swordplay, but* Khalifa *exponents protest that it is power of faith over flesh. Orthodox Muslims frown on this occultism.*

29. The silver dome of an old mosque contrasts with the concrete precision of the new Cape Town.

31

32

30. *Sombre in their mourning black, these women weep at a graveside.*

31. *A Malay choir, the Primrose Singkoor, performs with the band of the South African Navy. The music of the Cape Malays is one of the most interesting cultural features of the country. In it there are traces of Oriental and Hottentot music, Arab dances from Zanzibar, old Dutch folksongs, and the echoes of primitive stringed instruments that preceded the modern guitar. Their rollicking picnic songs, ghomma-* *liedjies, and narrative songs have had a marked influence on the folk music of the Afrikaner. In music the contact and mingling of cultures in South Africa is clearly apparent.*

32. *Rapt attention among the young girls and boys at a* madressa, *a school where the morals, history and worship of Islam are taught.*

33. The Marina da Gama housing scheme beside a lake on the shores of False Bay is a place where the affluent are able to escape the cluttered city sprawl.

34. It took almost 135 years for the Cape to advance from the mud-walled, thatch-roofed hovels of the first free burghers to this house, the Tokai manor-house designed by the famous Louis Michel Thibault. Extensively restored, it is now a historical monument.

35. From their history lessons these schoolgirls will learn of the sustained impact that English-speaking South Africans have had on the development of this country. Only slightly less numerous than the Afrikaners, who came to power earlier this century, the English-speaking population remains a pervasive force in many spheres. At the beginning of the 19th century English-speaking settlers challenged the British authorities at the Cape to entrench the ideas of the Age of Reason; John Fairbairn, Thomas Pringle and others like them fought for the rule of law and

34

35

freedom of speech, while James Rose-Innes founded the first countrywide educational system and a university. The literary traditions of English-speaking South Africans like Olive Schreiner and Percy FitzPatrick are today maintained by writers such as Nadine Gordimer, Laurens van der Post and Athol Fugard. And the news reports sent out by South Africa's English-speaking journalists are still an important medium through which an image of South Africa is presented to the world.

36

36. *For White South Africans, as far as the thorn tree country of the north, Cape Town long set the cultural standards – in architecture and art, in literature and gracious living. The Mother City never surrendered her authority to any rival, not even to the Golden Rand.*

37. *Queen Victoria's statue outside the Houses of Parliament in Cape Town recalls the days when South Africa consisted of two British colonies, the Cape and Natal, and two Boer republics, the Transvaal and the Orange Free State. Early constitutional history is essentially that of white colonists striving for more say in the running of the country – for freedom from Amsterdam and Downing Street – indeed, it was not until 1872 that the Cape Colony received the grant of self-government. Then the Anglo-Boer War of 1899-1902 brought South Africa under the British flag, though leaving it politically divided. In 1910 the four provinces chose union rather than federation. But in Parliament itself were heard constant constitutional arguments as Afrikaners, whose first Volksraad (House of Assembly) had met at Thaba Nchu in 1836, pursued the ideal of a republic. They achieved it in 1961 – and today the challenge is to satisfy black aspirations.*

38. *Social history is as indelibly traced in this Victorian cast iron as in any written record of events. The British, from the first British Occupation in 1795 to the present day, exerted a strong cultural influence. It is therefore not surprising that when the ostrich feather barons of Oudtshoorn and the gold magnates of the Reef chose an architectural style to reflect their new riches, they should favour lacy ironwork – ordered from a catalogue and shipped out from England as ballast in sailing ships!*

39. *The new Baxter Theatre complex proclaims in brick and glass and steel an international breadth of vision in its architecture – and in the music, ballet and theatre presented within its walls.*

37 38

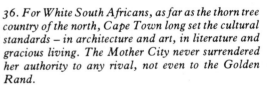

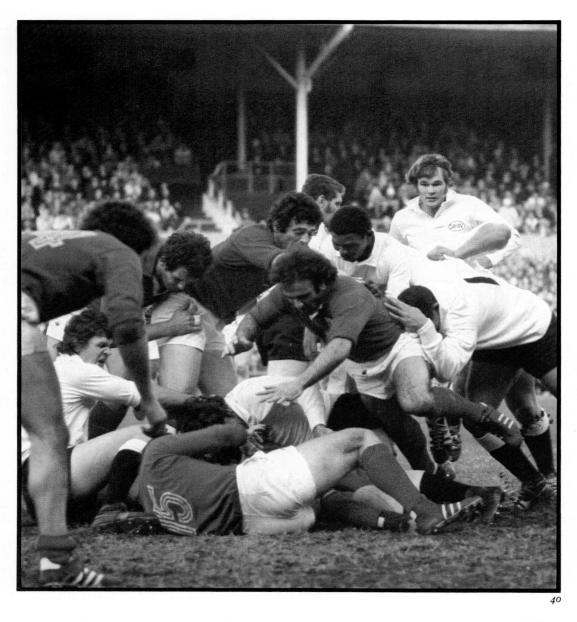

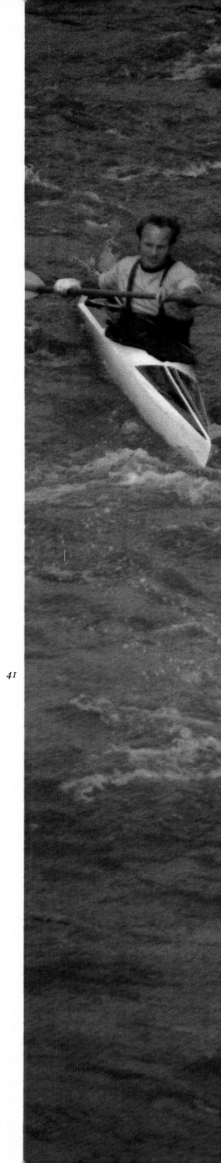

40. *Rugby is South Africa's tough national sport.*

41. *A game ranger started canoe racing in 1952 down the wild gorges of the Umgeni River which flows through Natal's spectacular Valley of a Thousand Hills. Since then, as this scene on the Cape's picturesque Berg River shows, the sport has caught on wherever there is good water.*

42   43

44   45

42. *Buying cultivars at the annual auction at Paarl is serious business for Cape wine farmers. In Europe farmers say the Good Lord makes the wine; in South Africa man must intervene to create the right conditions. But the end fully justifies the means: in general South Africa's best red wines compare favourably with Europe's noble vintages, and her superior sherries, ports and brandies with the finest in the world.*

43. *The golden sheen of autumn's grape harvest. Fifty years after Van Riebeeck's fleet had anchored in Table Bay, farmers were planting vines in distant Cape valleys. If the Portuguese limestone* padrãos *(crosses) planted at isolated points along the shores announced the coming of the European to southern Africa, then the vineyards and wheatfields showed that he was determined to stay.*

44. *Profits from good wines have built stately homes, their cool interiors adorned with Dutch delftware cherished for generations.*

45. *Preserved and lovingly burnished, the brass fittings on the door of the Tulbagh Church where the people below the Witzenberg offer up thanks for the good earth's bounty.*

46

47

46. *Set among vineyards, Lanzerac Estate just out-side Stellenbosch. The founding of Stellenbosch, the second oldest town in South Africa, marked the first step inland of the white migration that eventually reached the Limpopo River far to the north – a trek across mountain, veld and bush equal to a third of the distance across the United States of America.*

47. *Embodiment of the gracious Cape, the wine cellar of Vergelegen, a farm laid out in 1700 for his own benefit by the Dutch Governor Willem Adriaan van der Stel. Far from being a colonial treasure chest, the Cape was at first a heavy drain on the finances of the Dutch East India Company. Disgraced for his venality, Van der Stel nevertheless left in Vergelegen a memorial of great beauty.*

48

49

48. *There is geographical magic in the sudden transformation of the Karoo scrub and dust, when the traveller comes down the mountain pass that leads into vineyards with Cape Dutch farmhouses set in lyric green along the Hex River Valley – the vale of the witch. This is the border of the Boland, the country of the grape and winter rains, where in 1659 Jan van Riebeeck himself first made wine. Vines at Constantia caught the sea breeze – and their wine was, in time, enjoyed by Napoleon and Alexander Dumas. And there was French expertise in the wine they sipped. In 1688 some 176 Huguenots, refugees to Holland from the persecution of Protestants by Louis XIV, were sent to the Cape and given farms there, mainly in the Stellenbosch and Franschhoek valleys. Not only in viticulture and wine-making did*

they have a profound influence on South Africa; they intermarried with the Dutch and adopted their language, bequeathing to modern Afrikaners names that abound, such as Fourie, Labuschagne, du Plessis, du Toit, le Roux, Viljoen, Marais, Joubert and de Villiers. They shared the country's triumphs and tribulations – including those of the wine industry, threatened in 1866 by the American vine louse, Phylloxera vestatrix, but saved by the grafting on of American disease-resistant rootstock. Since 1918 prices and exports have been controlled by a giant cooperative, the K.W.V. (Kooperatieve Wijnbouwers Vereniging van Zuid-Afrika, Beperkt) and the wine industry has become one of the success stories of South African agriculture.

49. Cottages of labourers on a wine farm in the fertile Devon Valley.

50

51

50. *A small boy stands dwarfed by the soaring columns of the Afrikaans Language Monument built in 1976 to commemorate its growth and development. The first book in embryonic Afrikaans was printed in 1861; by the turn of the century there were 92, and within the next 60 years the number increased to 13 000. Today Afrikaans is the only literature with a complete bibliography from the four remaining copies of the first book to the works presently coming off the press. In its infancy it had the grammatical simplicity of a vernacular; and although it has sought to avoid unnecessary assimilations from the almost universal English vocabulary, it is now faced with the need for terms to meet the demands of science and technology. Afrikaans, the youngest form of Germanic, took its place beside English in 1925 to become South Africa's second official language.*

51. *The coastlands near Caledon in the Overberg are sheep and wheat country. The Dutch sowed the first wheat in southern Africa on the 3rd of July 1652 and for two centuries the migration of the bread-eating white man was mainly directed to places where there was good rainfall or irrigation water for his patches of wheat.*

52. The green revolution of the Seventies is marching but slowly across the wheatfields of South Africa, and methods of production lag far behind those of the United States, but one salient fact emerges from the mass of statistics that has been compiled: she can still more than meet the food demands of her exploding population. Indeed the black rural areas, where today farmers using traditional means of cultivation barely subsist, have the potential, with optimum use of the natural resources, of feeding 35 million people.

54

53. *The wheatfields of the Cape west coast are small compared with those of the American Great Plains – but the whole of Africa, second largest continent, produces less than 4% of the world's wheat. In years of good rainfall South Africa is self-sufficient.*

54. *A farm labourer stacks bags of wheat in the Cape. South African agriculture depends on black labour to the extent that by 1979 there will be 29 black workers for every one white on the land.*

55

56

57

58

59

The wild flowers of the Cape Floral Kingdom are of great beauty and unique botanical interest. Their setting, the fynbos, consists of a multitude of species that astounded botanists like Anders Sparrman and Carl Thunberg who in 1772 sent specimens to the great Linnaeus. The master described the Cape of Good Hope as a paradise on earth, more valuable than the wealth of Solomon or Croesus. There are more than 16 000 species of flowering plants in South Africa and in the Cape Peninsula alone there are at least 2 600 – more than in the whole of Great Britain. The origin of the fynbos has long been a mystery. In 1881 Charles Darwin guessed that this flora might have come from a lost southern continent, now known as Gondwanaland, for the species composition was so great that it could hardly have evolved in one small corner of Africa. Perhaps the riddle will be solved by new methods of studying fossil pollens. Meanwhile the beauty of these 'flowers from nowhere' is there for all the world to admire.

60

61 62

63

55. The blushing bride protea (Serruria florida).

56. Erica cyranthoides.

57. Erica physoides.

58. Erica bauera.

59. Erica blerina.

60. Aulax umbellata.

61. The pincushion (Leucospermum cordifolium).

62. Erica mammosa.

63. Helicrysum vestitum.

64
66
70

65
68
71   72

69
73

64. *The lovely marsh rose* (Orothamnus zeyheri) *was one of the rarest plants in the world in 1967 when only nine plants, six of them dying, were known. Rescue work by botanists succeeded in saving the species and there are now 300 flourishing in a Cape nursery.*

74

65. *Woolly-bearded protea* (Protea magnifia).

66. Littonia modesta.

67. Disa uniflora.

68. Leucospermum tottum.

69. Dietes iridioides.

70. Gladiolus carneus.

71. Protea witsenbergiana.

72. Lachnaea filamentosa.

73. Protea eximia.

74. Protea cynaroides, *the King Protea, is South Africa's floral emblem.*

75. *Billowing smoke settles over Sir Lowry's Pass as a Garrat locomotive puffs up to Elgin's apple country. Between February and May the aroma of ripe apples is mixed with that of steam and smoke as trains in almost continual procession haul the apple harvest over the pass and down to Cape Town docks for export to the fruit markets of the world. This railway line reaches still further eastward to the Overberg where white colonists began farming in the 18th century and rapidly loosened their bonds with the Dutch East India Company, which sought to control every aspect of the lives of the settlers at the Cape.*

76. *Safe and scenic, the Montagu Pass over the Outeniqua Mountains bears scant resemblance to the dreaded Cradock Pass which it replaced. The early passes usually followed game trails used by Hottentot nomads traversing the rugged mountains of the Cape.*

77. *Sunshine and unsurpassed natural beauty make South Africans keen sportsmen and great lovers of the outdoor life.*

78   79

78. Bontebok (pied buck) were once found in fair numbers in the coastal regions of the southern and south-eastern Cape, but by 1900 hunting had made them the rarest species of antelope in the world. The effective measures taken since then to ensure their protection represent an epic in the saga of world conservation.

79. A small farm in the Overberg where the fynbos thins out and wheat and sheep replace the vineyard. This area marks the second step of the white migration inland away from Dutch East India Company control. In 1795 Swellendam saw armed patriots establish a national assembly and heard slogans of the French Revolution. In this lay the germinal concept of an Afrikaner nation, a people committed to their country and owing allegiance to no other. These people were first known to the world as 'the Boers' – agrarian, deeply religious and patriarchal in character; and the vision that guided them was that of a people in search of a country and freedom.

80. *Arniston, a tiny rather dilapidated fishing village near Cape Agulhas. Many of the essential features of Cape architecture are evident in these simple white-washed cottages, plans for whose restoration have focused fresh interest on the plight of the community of coloured fishermen who battle the elements to make a meagre living from the sea.*

81. *Local women clean and gut the day's catch. Trek-fishing from beaches and inshore bottom-fishing still yield a harvest for the coloured families who have been fishing this coast for generations. However, many of the men now seek work on the big offshore seiners and bottom-trawlers, responding inevitably to the lure of better money.*

82

83

82. *The warm blue waters of the Agulhas Current attract thousands of inland visitors to Plettenberg Bay, where accommodation varies from the most luxurious of hotels to simple campsites overlooking the breakers. But the beauty of this area is not restricted to the coastline. The interior reveals magnificent forest land. From here stinkwood was first exported to the East for craftsmen to fashion table legs with the traditional ball and claw feet.*

83. *A true marine wilderness, where man must tread gently and with reverence on sands that stretch in golden solitude as far as the eye can see.*

84

84. *Visitors are warmly welcomed on the lonely farms. In the* voorkamers *(drawing rooms) there are tales of drought and hardship, of crop prices and community events, there is nostalgia for relatives long dead at war, and pride in children gone to live in the towns. Surrounded by memories and alive with hope,* this is the heart of the heartland of South Africa's conservative Afrikaner society. In spite of rapid urbanisation, there are still 80 000 farming units in the rural areas and most Afrikaners preserve their links with the land by regularly visiting friends and relatives still on the farms.

85. *The tang of resin in the air, a sawyer and his assistant watch the blades bite as logs pass through a mill.*

86. *A pair of Yellow-billed Egrets, their elegant plumage tossed by the breeze. This bird rarely hunts away from water, and so its distribution mirrors the migratory movements of black and white peoples in southern Africa as they, too, followed the rivers and waterholes.*

87. *Known for its graceful tail and its call like a tiny ripple of laughter, a Paradise Flycatcher tends its hungry brood. High up in a tree the well-formed nest is adorned with lichens for camouflage.*

88 89
90 91

92

88–91. *Stretching for some 80 kilometres along the Knysna shore is the Tsitsikama Coastal Park, a protected coastline of rugged majesty – and of special interest to marine scientists. Here two great ocean currents meet; the warm Agulhas Current that flows from the Tropics; and the cold Benguela Current that sweeps up from the Antarctic. Where they come together the sea supports a rich combination of endemic species with those of the east and west coasts. In the tidal pools (89) there is a teeming diversity of life such as the familiar flowerlike sea anemone, its name from the Greek word for wind (88), and the starfish found in every ocean (90), to strange creatures like these giant fanworms (91) that seem the product of evolution gone beserk.*

92. *Classified by world conservationists as a unique natural area, the Storms River is born in mountain mists, courses through deep gorges that took aeons to erode and dies in the Indian Ocean breakers of the Tsitsikama coast (right). Its catchment is the habitat of a splendour of trees and flowers, of butterflies and birds and small mammals of the underbrush.*

93. *Thirty metres below the lofty canopy of ironwood, yellowwood, assegai and stinkwood, there is the green calm of the underbrush of the Tsitsikama Forest – South Africa's oldest tree sanctuary. This country has not been endowed by nature with vast forests and the pioneer farmers, unlike those of Europe and America, did not have to clear woodland to make houses and ships, ploughs and waterwheels, wagons and furniture. The smack of the axe first echoed in the Tsitsikama in 1630 when sailors from the wreck São Gonçales built two boats to escape along the coast; and in time the need for timber made woodcutters the advance-guard of exploitation. Only very much later were there laws and plans to protect what was left of the big trees. Today only 143 400 hectares of tall forest remains. Fast-growing exotics were planted in Worcester in 1876 to fuel the railway locomotives and today these forests – mainly pines and eucalypts – have been introduced as far north as the Soutpansberg. They cover over a million hectares and supply 90% of the country's timber needs.*

94

95

94. A tableau of society in transition: steel frame windows and a rectangular-plan brick house replace the familiar mud-walled rondavel, while in the foreground an ox-drawn wagon reflects the relatively recent advent of the wheel to southern Africa. These grasslands of the Eastern Cape marked the southern-most migration of Xhosa-speaking people. Increasing population has dictated events in Africa as surely as its present world explosion will affect this planet in decades to come. In central Africa, long before the birth of Christ, when an area became overpopulated there was conflict and those who lost their claim to the land moved on. And so the process repeated itself, again and again, like a game until the black man had reached as far south as the Fish River in the eastern Cape and 200 years ago met the white man moving north, impelled by the same territorial imperatives and just as hungry for land. But by then there was no longer the alternative of moving on. Initially there were skirmishes and confrontations as people, black and white, manoeuvred for position. Today the board is set, each player is restricted in his moves and the quest for survival takes on new complexity. While the black population of South Africa now explodes at an unprecedented rate, available land remains fixed. And in the final analysis it will be the natural limitations that call the play. Running north-south, at an angle to the coast, is the 375mm isohyet which effectively demarcates the limitations of the land; west of this fragile line lies inhospitable semi-desert; to the east the well-watered 'Blue' Triangle – less than 47% of the whole and, with the Cape, the area to which South Africans, both black and white, must limit their dreams. Deprived of the alternative of more space, the players must be ever more ingenious and productive to maintain their growing populations.

95. Spirits inhabit the valleys – or so popular belief goes among many of the Xhosa-speaking peoples whose homesteads traditionally cling to the hilltops and ridges. Here, the rolling landscape of the Eastern Cape provides ideal living conditions: open grass-land for the herds, land for the crops, trees in the valleys for firewood, and water near by.

96

96. Splendidly attired in their swathed headdresses and intricate beadwork, Xhosa-speaking girls clap and sing while the men perform at a Sunday afternoon dance. Naked breasts proclaiming their unmarried status, the girls have come to banter and flirt with the eligible bachelors of the district. Traditional African marriage bears a closer resemblance to the arranged marriages of European dynasties than to the contemporary western form. It is essentially a family affair in which relatives of the bride and groom negotiate the transfer of goods and, traditionally, cattle, from the man's family to that of the woman. Lobola, the cornerstone of traditional marriage, has been widely misinterpreted as a crude form of bride purchase. In fact, among all the black peoples of South Africa, bridewealth not only legitimises the union, but provides safeguards and ensures certain rights for both parties. However, here as in most other aspects of traditional life, marriage is undergoing change: not necessarily in the complete rejection of old ways but in the acceptance of a new reality that lies somewhere in between. Nowadays, for instance, a couple may marry out of free choice and have a church wedding. Yet the groom may still send gifts of money and blankets to his new wife's family and in the marriage there will be a synthesis of obligations old and new.

97

97. *White clay smeared on the face of the Xhosa initiate (umkwetha) sets him apart from the rest of the community while he undergoes the transition to manhood. The seclusion of adolescent boys from the community, their circumcision, and surrounding the ceremony with ritual and secrecy is their dramatic and indelible introduction to the tenets and values of adult society.*

98. *These cheerful water-carriers know that in Xhosa tribal life it is the lot of the women to do most of the hard work, not only in the hut or around the cooking fire, but in hoeing the fields and planting the crops.*

99. *Neat little houses laid out with the mathematical precision of a surveyor's grid say much of the black man's transition from peasant farmer with his fields and herds close by his hut to landless unit in the labour force.*

100. *It was the white man who brought tobacco and the pipe as well as cloth for huge headdresses into the fashion world of Xhosa women.*

102

101. *Women were the slaves of* iLembe, *the hoe, from the time this digging implement appeared in southern Africa long before the birth of Christ. When the seven stars of the Pleiades,* isiLimela, *rose in the eastern morning sky, the planting season began and the more wives a man had, the greater his labour force. But the agricultural revolution which saw the plough gradually replace the hoe, needed men to drive the oxen, and the traditional division of labour began to undergo subtle change. Here a Pondo woman, her hair stretched and lengthened with thread, strides home along the white sands of the Wild Coast, her hoe slung over her shoulder.*

102. *The headdresses of married women are distinctive and differ from group to group. After marriage, the new bride traditionally leaves her father's homestead and goes to live with her husband's family. Out of respect for her father-in-law and new relatives her headdress is worn low over her face and only after she has borne a child does her status improve.*

103. *An unselfconscious face-lift for a building on a dusty village street.*

104. *Hanging round a rural postbox, these boys dream of the day when they will be part of a bigger world. The tales they hear of life in the towns, of underground shifts and motor cars, of money to be made and pleasures to be bought, of clothes and transistor radios and assembly lines, these all filter back by way of mouth. But by post comes money, sent by fathers and brothers, to the women and children and elderly left on the land. With it will be bought new hoes, cooking pots, blankets and food – the necessities of life which are beyond the resources of the women left behind on their smallholdings.*

105. Port Elizabeth in the Eastern Cape is as British as the Western Cape is Dutch. Enduring traces of its origins are found in the Edwardian art nouveau style of public buildings and in the Victorian-Georgian-Settler houses with their wooden verandahs and balconies. Here, houses with English-style terraces are stepped down to Algoa Bay where 4 000 Settlers on 21 British transports landed in the first half of 1820 – unaware that they were to be a buffer in the much-disputed Zuurveld to keep the blacks on the far side of the Fish River boundary. Their small farms on sandy soil, where rust attacked the wheat, could not produce a viable crop-raising settlement; so half of them soon left the land. Some bartered ivory, others set up trade stores that spread western goods and ideas among the blacks. The Dutch-speaking grensboere (border farmers), hitherto almost self-sufficient, also began to trade ostrich feathers, ox-hides, tallow and soap for British manufactured goods. In Britain the industrial revolution spread from cotton factories to Yorkshire's woollen mills, and Settlers who had bought bigger farms introduced merino sheep whose fleeces became the Cape's chief export by 1840. Indeed, the Settlers' contribution of a rich economic heritage to South Africa far exceeded the initial purpose for which they were brought out.

106. The people who lived in these houses with their elaborately worked balconies, brought English culture and tradition to South Africa as well as new methods of trading and agriculture. Grahamstown was to many English-speaking South Africans what Stellenbosch was to the Afrikaners. By sharing frontier hardships and wars the two white language groups were drawn more closely together here than in any other region of South Africa. The Eastern Cape is the true melting-pot where Hottentot, Xhosa, Boer and Briton disputed ownership of the land, fought, died, disappeared from the scene – or slowly adapted to a new South Africa.

107. Before roads and communication links came to span its semi-arid expanses, the Great Karoo was as much of an obstacle to the wagons of the migrating whites as the oceans had been to the sailing ships that brought them from Europe. But first they had to cross the gentler Little Karoo, seen here with the flowers of fynbos fading perhaps like the trekkers' memories of the vineyards and wild almond hedges of the Cape.

108. A lonely Karoo store, centre of commerce in this sparsely populated area where the next farm always appears to be beyond the distant horizon of table-top kopjes (hills).

109
110
111

109. *Windmills are the main feature of a Karoo town, and the thud of the windpumps is often all that breaks the night silence. At Sutherland the observatory draws astronomers from all over the world; for here, 1 456 metres above sea-level and without smog or humidity to veil the skies, the vista of the heavens is incomparably revealed.*

110. *Some seven thousand coloureds live in this picturesque if dusty village on the outskirts of Graaff-Reinet.*

111. *A green and white oasis in a Karoo-brown setting, Graaff-Reinet is South Africa's third oldest country town and an outpost of Cape architecture and lifestyle. In the early years of the settlement the gun often supplanted the spade, and frontier clashes with the Xhosa and Bushman steeled the resolve of the burghers (citizens) to rebel against the authorities at the Cape. From here, in the same spirit of independence, Gerrit Maritz's wagon party moved off in August 1836 to join the Great Trek – the white migration that thrust deep into the heart of the country.*

113

114

112

115

112. *It takes two engines to bring the Mossel Bay-Johannesburg express over the high Lootsberg Pass, seen here under snow.*

113. *In company with the quaggas which were hunted to extinction, large flocks of ostriches once roamed the Karoo. But they were spared the same fate when they were tamed in the 1860s and farmed on a large scale to meet the overseas demand for ostrich feathers. The open motor-car brought about a change in women's fashions and in 1914 the booming feather industry went into a decline.*

114. *The Cango Caves are among the most spectacular natural wonders of South Africa. Discovered by chance in 1780 during a search for lost cattle, their marvel lies not so much in their size as in the wealth of formations and the abundance of their natural colours. The ones presently accessible extend for more than 800 metres underground; but new and exciting finds promise even greater splendours beyond.*

115. *Colesberg Kopje stands like a beacon on the northern boundary of the arid Karoo.*

116

117

116. An early traveller, John Centlivres Chase, in 1842 described the Karoo as ' . . . doomed by nature to remain unfruitful wildernesses'. He wrote: 'A constant mirage haunts for ever the thirsty traveller on these blasted heaths . . . wherever the eye roams are the continual, monotonous and tantalising phenomena of this inhospitable solitude.' Nature herself made the Karoo an arid grassland, parched but for rare torrents that tear the earth and wash away its topsoil in tawny floodwaters. But its scarred landscape holds features which give it as great a claim to fame as the steppes of Europe and the prairies and pampas of the Americas: its rocks reveal the fossil record of the slow transition from reptile to mammal and of the evolution of the drifting continents themselves. More recently the white man and black destroyed the Bushman of the Karoo in order to occupy his ecological niche – the water-holes where the herds of game came to drink. In this inhospitable land, scorched by the west wind, it was the borehole and windpump that enabled man to settle with his herds of merino sheep.

117. Typical of the Karoo – the donkey cart and the seemingly interminable dirt road. Experts fear that desert encroachment from the west may turn the region into a stony pavement and march on over the Orange River into grasslands and maize fields as far as the Vaal River in the north. The Karoo already constitutes almost a third of South Africa's total land surface.

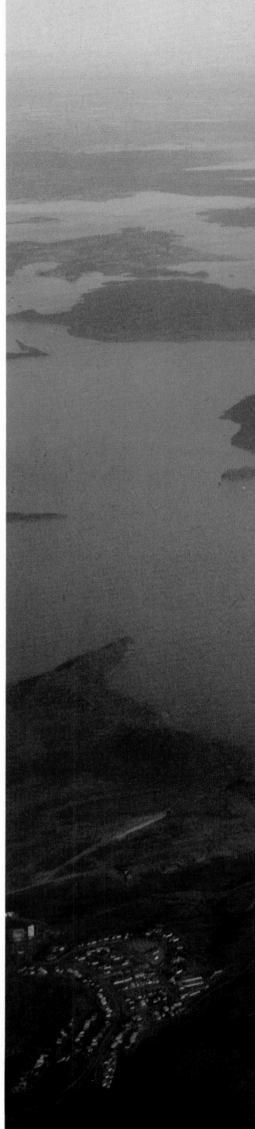

118   119

118. *A vast expanse for water sport was suddenly created when the largest storage reservoir in the country, the Hendrik Verwoerd Dam, was built in a narrow gorge of the Orange River. Shortage of water over much of the country and the inconsistency of the rainfall have been limiting factors in her development. About 60% of the country receives less than 500 mm a year and even in relatively well-watered areas, years of drought may follow years of flood.*

119. *The Hendrik Verwoerd Dam's gravity-and-arch type wall controls the wild and fickle flow of the Orange River's average yearly run-off of 6 500 million cubic metres. The great floods from the mountain catchments of the Drakensberg course 2 250 kilometres westwards across the face of South Africa before being lost to the Atlantic Ocean. In harnessing this resource, precious in a dry country, turbines produce electricity and canals feed water to new and ambitious irrigation schemes. The Orange River Project, of which this dam is but part, demonstrated South Africa's technical ability to develop the wealth of her resources.*

120

121

122

120-122. When it rains the flowers still bloom in Namaqualand, but the Nama Hottentots who gave the land its name are all but forgotten. They live on only in the bloodlines of coloureds treading dusty roads where once their ancestors watched the wagon trains of 17th century explorers in search of the Kingdom of Monomotapa, the copper mountain of early reports, and the fabled city of Vigiti Magna. It was the scientists of later generations who lifted the lid of Namaqualand's treasure chest: the copper mines at Okiep; diamonds hidden in the ancient rock terraces at the mouth of the Orange River; and at Aggenys in the north-east where all is now ready to mine one of the biggest deposits of base minerals in the whole of the Republic of South Africa.

123

124

123. In the Cedarberg, where the highest peaks rise to some 2 063 metres, the Wolfberg is noted for its remarkable formations, crevices and arches.

124. Fine-wool merino sheep now graze as far inland as Namaqualand, supplanting the indigenous fat-tailed species.

125. In the large loop made by the Orange River before it enters the sea lie the granite highlands of the Richtersveld, where the Hottentot deity Heitsi Eibib watches over his treasure from a dreaded cave, the Wondergat. In this sere wasteland live 2 000 coloured people scattered over 512 600 hectares.

127 128

129 130

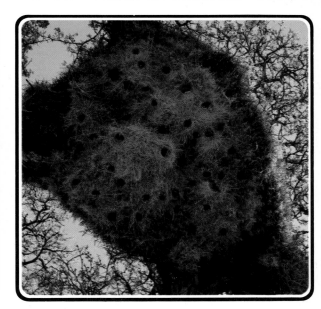

126 131 132

126. *Augrabies – 'the water that thunders'. The Koranas, nomadic Hottentots, who named this granite gorge where the Orange River plunges, shared the widespread belief among black people that the roar of the waterfall is the birthplace of thunder.*

127. *Except when coaxed into flower by rain, the Dinteranthus wilmotianus is difficult to detect. Its highly reduced leaves mimic the colour and texture of its desert habitat, making the plant less readily visible to grazing animals.*

128. *The African lynx or rooikat* (Felis caracal).

129. *Tritonia flava is the desert cousin of the familiar hybridized members of the iris family.*

130. *The deadly Cape Cobra or Geelkapel.*

131. *This unusual succulent,* Ophthalmophyllum mauchanii, *is an extreme adaptation to desert conditions – only the tips of the leaves peer above ground.*

132. *Such are the skills of the Social Weaver that its great tenement-block nests have been known to remain in continuous use for a century or more.*

134

133. *The end of a journey that began at Sishen over 800 kilometres inland – the ore-loading quay at Saldanha Bay. The decision to invest about R700-million in the Sishen/Saldanha project created a new economic growth-point at the Cape, and signalled the exploitation of one of South Africa's great base mineral deposits. The open-pit iron-ore mine at Sishen* *has long supplied the state-owned Iron and Steel Corporation (Iscor), but reserves were such that an ambitious export scheme was feasible. This undertaking required the construction of facilities to handle the loading of millions of tonnes of ore at Saldanha, and a new railway-line linking the mine with the harbour.*

134. *High-grade haematite spews from an ore tippler at Saldanha Bay. Eventually the scheme will be expanded to handle the immense wealth of the North West Cape, and copper, manganese, lead, zinc and magnetite will follow the route of Sishen's ore to the industrial centres of the world.*

135

136

135. *Coloured fishermen reap the abundance of fish that feed on plankton in the cold upwelling waters of the Benguela Current along the west coast. They have helped build a mighty industry – one of the eleven biggest in the world – with millions of tonnes of fish caught every year until the shoals, like the herds of game on the land, were endangered.*

136. *Lambert's Bay is jammed with dories engaged in the tightly-controlled crayfish industry. The valuable catch is sold mainly in America as South African rock-lobster. In the background are the trawlers that follow the once-great shoals of pilchards, the basis of the presentday coastal fishing industry. The arrival of trawlers of many nations to plunder this rich area is the cause of still unresolved disputes over limitations of catches and the extent of territorial waters.*

137

137. Along the treeless west coast, a wooden boat rests on the slipway at Velddrift, a fishing village at the mouth of the Berg River.

138. *The cold Benguela Current that brings the shoals of fish also dictates the climate of Africa's west coast from the Cape to the Equator. Inland lies desert, not true desert but the Kalahari thirstlands that extend north to the Zambezi in the largest continuous mantle of sand in the world. Where the rainfall is lowest there are dunes, bare but for hardy grasses and trees that have adapted to the environment. This part of the country is a virtual population vacuum – even the Bushman is rarely seen here; most of these small hunter-gatherers live in the semi-desert areas of Botswana and Namibia.*

141

142

139. *Pioneer desert vegetation defies red sands, each grain tinted with a pellicle of iron oxide that shows the absence of moisture.*

140. *Like a squadron of lancers a herd of gemsbok (Oryx gazella) move with nodding heads through well-grassed Kalahari veld.*

141. *Change is coming to the Kalahari Bushman and its impact is clearly reflected in his camp. Mobility and adaptability have for thousands of years ensured his survival. But the borehole and the trading store, tobacco and the cooking pot, have begun to* entice *him from his desert fastnesses. New possessions have stolen from him the mobility that allowed this hunter-gatherer to follow the game spoors and shift camp across the sands. Of the estimated 50 000 defined by language and physical features as Bushmen, only some 2 000 cling to the age-old way of life in which man and nature live in perfect harmony.*

142. *Vital in the life of the Bushman hunter: the bow for meat, the life-giving moisture of the tsamma melon (partially obscured by sand), and water stored in buried ostrich eggs.*

143

144

145

146

143. *A herd of ostriches, like models for a decorative frieze of Bushman rock paintings, run with seven-league strides across a denuded Kalahari plain.*

144. *The lion is the first to be hunted when cattle ranchers bring their herds to a new area.*

145. *Creatures of an arid land, ground squirrels dig with powerful claws for roots and bulbs. These gregarious rodents often live in large colonies and can be seen perched upright at the mouths of their burrows.*

146. *The wildebeest has less tolerance for thirst than other large animals of the Kalahari and during the dry season the herds may travel 40 kilometres or more a day to drink.*

147. *The swift and timid cheetah has been relentlessly hunted down for its coat.*

148. *White-faced Owls, birds of the acacia savannah, perch on thorn trees until the hours of darkness when they feed.*

149. *The majestic Secretary Bird attacks snakes with blows from its feet and then rips at its prey with its beak. The bird carefully checks whether the snake is dead before swallowing it — sometimes whole.*

150. *Plains of Africa's only great plateau, the High-veld where dust-devils whirl in winter but spring rains bring out the wonder of its grasses.*

147

148

149

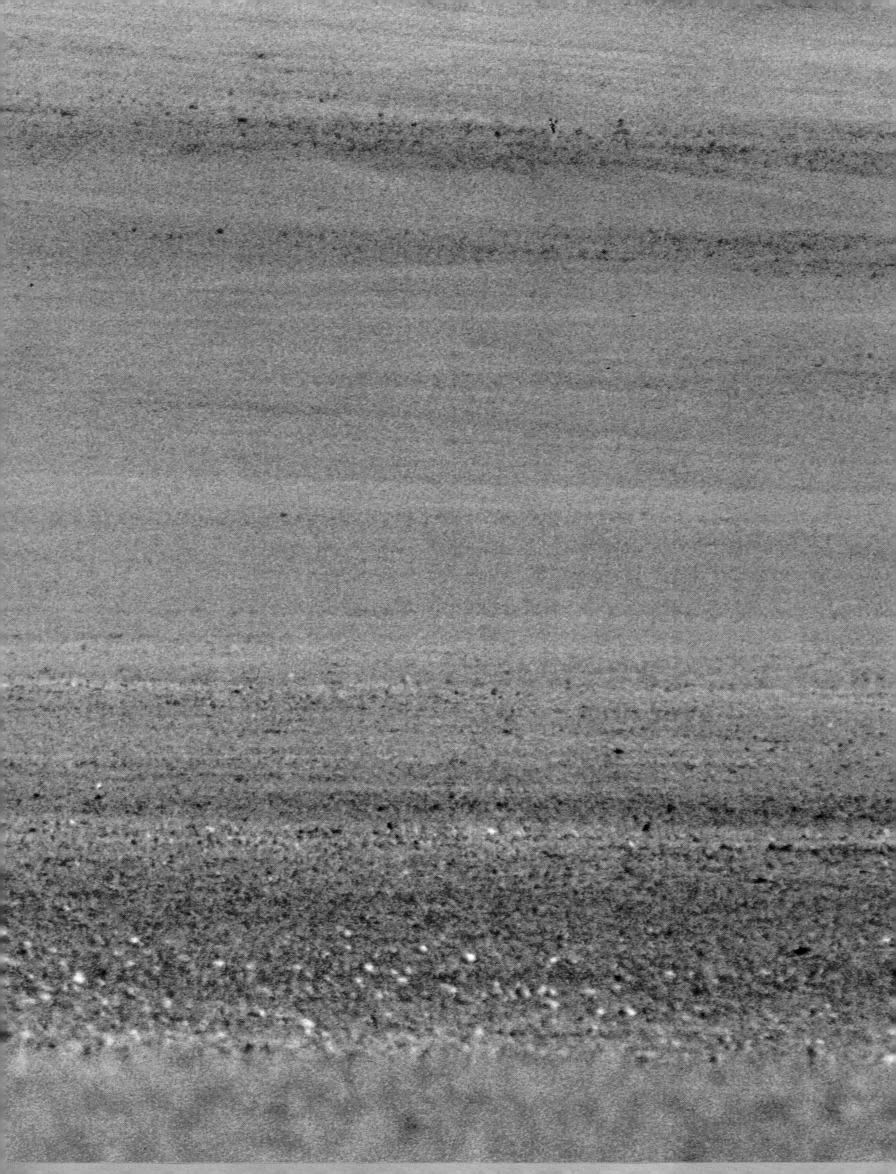

154. *Exotic trees are signposts that point to the first white homesteads of the Highveld. In the wagon-boxes there were acorns and pips of peaches and apricots; oaks grew beside the water-furrows and willows round the dams, while avenues of stately poplars marked the approach roads to farms. Australian eucalypts and wattles came later to make shade for the stock and supply firewood to the home. Tree-planting was a new idea in Africa and it changed the Highveld landscape.*

155. *When barbed wire was patented in 1862 the herdboy began to disappear. He was replaced by camps for rotational grazing, and the farm gate between fenced pastures.*

156. *Highways radiate from the nucleus of economic activity, the Witwatersrand, where mines and industry generate most of the country's wealth.*

157. *Sunflowers, natives of North America, stretch out to the horizon. They have become an important crop of the Highveld and are the basis of a large edible-oil and cattle fodder industry.*

158. *Farm workers' houses of packed sods plastered with clay – the adobe of South Africa.*

159. *The first white man to work in the Transvaal was a missionary in 1823 and churches still labour actively in this field.*

156

157
158
159

160. *White pioneers brought many new things to the veld – the yoke to inspan oxen, the wagon and the gun, the plough and horses, donkeys and sheep. It was not long before the farm workers adopted these innovations on their own smallholdings: where women with hoes had planted the sorghum, a plough now turned the sod.*

161. *Most black men in the rural areas began life as herdboys – first of the goats and later, at about the age of ten, the cattle. In traditional society, a man's herd was his 'bank on the hoof' – a symbol of wealth and status far beyond its practical value as meat or milk.*

162. *A Sotho woman prepares the stooks of thatching grass which the chief traditionally distributes among his people. However, new architectural trends and changing values have diminished his role both as leader and as the regulating influence in the annual cycle. The Sotho peoples who number close on two million are made up of several groupings showing a large degree of cultural and linguistic uniformity.*

163. *More than a century has passed since Mzilikazi and his Ndebele warriors and Shaka's impis devastated this area and its peoples. Then the door was small and low so that an enemy had to crawl before he could enter a hut.*

164. *A congregant, dressed in church uniform, reads up tomorrow's lesson.*

160

161
162
163
164

165

165. This veld, where a peaceful shepherd now leads his flock, has been a huge stage for the drama of evolving life. Wild animals by the millions grazed here, and in its limestone caves fossil skulls have been found that staked Africa's claim to be the birthplace of the hominids. The archaeological record reveals how two million years ago apemen co-existed with Stone Age people. Then black peoples moved in with their herds and hoes and, not long before Europe heard Bach's music, displaced the last of the Stone Age hunters so that in southern Africa today only remnants of Stone Age culture survive in remote parts of the Kalahari.

166. A whole atlas of fantastic cloud formations opens up in summer Highveld skies. Thunderstorms and cloudbursts often pelt the veld with raindrops that leave the lacerations of sheet and donga erosion. Since the first plough tore the plains and cattle and sheep over-grazed the veld, South Africa has lost a quarter of the Highveld's most fertile topsoil.

166

167. *A farm in the prosperous agricultural area round Harrismith. The town was named after the dashing Governor of the Cape Colony, Sir Harry Smith, and it boomed during the Kimberley diamond rush of the 1860s. It became a regular stop for the transport wagons that toiled up the escarpment from Natal each day, bringing goods and equipment to the new mining town. And, when gold was found on the Witwatersrand, its hotels and stores became even busier. But, railways replaced the wagons and Harrismith is now a farming centre.*

168. *Cattle auctions are still important events in rural life, despite marketing control and price fixing in the meat industry. In 1977 the number of cattle in white areas reached a record peak of ten million head. There are about half that number in black areas.*

169. One of Van Riebeeck's top priorities when he came to the Cape was to barter with the Hottentots for cattle – and the beasts he obtained were far inferior to those which form the basis of South Africa's industry today. Three foundation types of African cattle, the Hamitic longhorn – the oldest African bovine, the Brachyceros or dwarf shorthorn type imported from Asia many years ago, and the Zebu or humped cattle which also came from Asia but more recently, are the basis of the very numerous breeds that exist today. Later, white ranchers imported foreign stock, but the beef industry in this country still depends largely on the Afrikander which is an improved breed of Zebu and excellently adapted to African climatic and grazing conditions.

170. *Genetic planning, five cross-breedings of the Spanish Escorial merino sheep with the* kaapse skaap *– the Cape sheep which the Dutch burghers inherited from the Hottentots – produced the* vaderlandsskaap *which had pure wool. But soon grazing habits of the new breed transformed much of the marginal grasslands into a semi-desert of succulent plants. Despite this, sheep farming remains a major industry which, during the 1976-77 season, earned South African farmers a total income of R162 million.*

171. *In the shadow of Table Mountain the first Dutch farmers tilled the Company's garden and then their own free-holdings. On the* vlaktes *of the North the pioneers lived off the veld which had produced the world's greatest biomass of game – vast herds of blesbok, springbok, black wildebeest, hartebeest and the huge eland. On the Highveld the hunter's gun helped fill the cooking pot until diamonds were found in the Vaal River and gold in reefs that outcropped along the 'Ridge of White Waters' – the Witwatersrand.*

172

*172. The trees that stand tall against this skyline
came to the Highveld from across the sea — Australian
eucalypts for the fence poles and Lombardy poplars
planted in rows.*

173

174

173. *Orchards of sweet cherries bloom in the cold Maluti Mountain country of the Orange Free State.*

174. *Afrikaners, wearing costumes of the Great Trek period, wait to perform traditional folk dances (volk-spele). The centenary of the Great Trek in 1936 marked the beginning of an Afrikaner cultural revival that found expression in dress and a near veneration of the ox-wagon. Some 60% of South Africa's white population are Afrikaners – descendants of the people who had crossed the vlaktes to escape authority imposed from across the sea and in the process became men of Africa forever.*

175. *Dutch Reformed churches, often resembling the one in Geneva where John Calvin preached, dominate the South African village, architecturally and psychologically. Here, at Ladybrand, the church steeple marks the heart of the town.*

176

177 178

179

176. *In remoter areas where initiation is still some-times practised, Sotho boys and girls have to endure considerable hardship in the course of their transition to adulthood. This Sotho initiate is wearing dress that sets her apart from society, and for the several months that she attends the secret Bale school she will be instructed in matters relating to domestic activities and sex so that with other girls in her group she will rejoin society well equipped to fulfil her adult rôle.*

177. *Early morning in the mountain foothills brings sunlight to a stone-built Sotho hut.*

178. *Muted earth tones on the wall of a hut.*

179. *A Sotho beauty wears the blanket much fa-voured in the rural districts by both men and women. The blanket-pin, too, is a popular innovation, but beads have a long history in Africa; from the bedrock of Zimbabwe to those sold by the trading stores today, beads are valuable clues to the past culture of the black peoples.*

180

182

181

180. Villages and smallholdings loop in a green belt round the Witwatersrand, South Africa's great metropolitan complex. Only three out of every 20 hectares of the country's land surface are arable, and 90% has been ploughed already.

181, 182. Johannesburg, born less than a century ago, was soon scarred with the ugly signs of rapid growth. But planners gave the Golden City cosmetic treatment by setting aside parks and open spaces.

183   184

183. Washing festoons this 'location in the sky' – rooftop housing for black domestic workers in Johannesburg.

184. Dates and names on weathered tombstones record something of the early history of the Witwatersrand. Certainly the discovery of its rich banket formation in 1886 was the culmination of years of sporadic searching for gold in the Transvaal and in the alluvial diggings of Pilgrim's Rest, Lydenburg and Barberton which attracted wandering prospectors reared on the gold rushes of California and New South Wales. More controversial is the question as to who really discovered gold here – and for that matter who was the 'Johannes' immortalised in the naming of the city. But they are irrelevent in terms of history for it was the entrepreneurial skills of others with names like Barnato, Rhodes and Oppenheimer who exploited the riches of the gold and diamond mines and in the process set the course for South Africa's remarkable industrial development.

185. The skyline of Johannesburg, picked out in lights against a dark and stormy sky. A photograph taken in 1885 – the year before gold was discovered – of the area where the city now stands, would have shown nothing but tall grass and barren upland. In the 90 years since gold began pouring from the crucibles of the Rand, Johannesburg has grown from a roisterous shanty town to a mighty city.

186

187

188

189

186-190. Commerce came north to the source of wealth. Plush shopping centres cater for suburban whites but do not necessarily reflect the trends seen in the sprawling black townships where there is a taste in dress for things American and the emphasis is on quality.

191-193. For an ever-increasing number of urban blacks ties with a traditional rural background have lost relevance and they seek recognition of their rights as urban citizens.

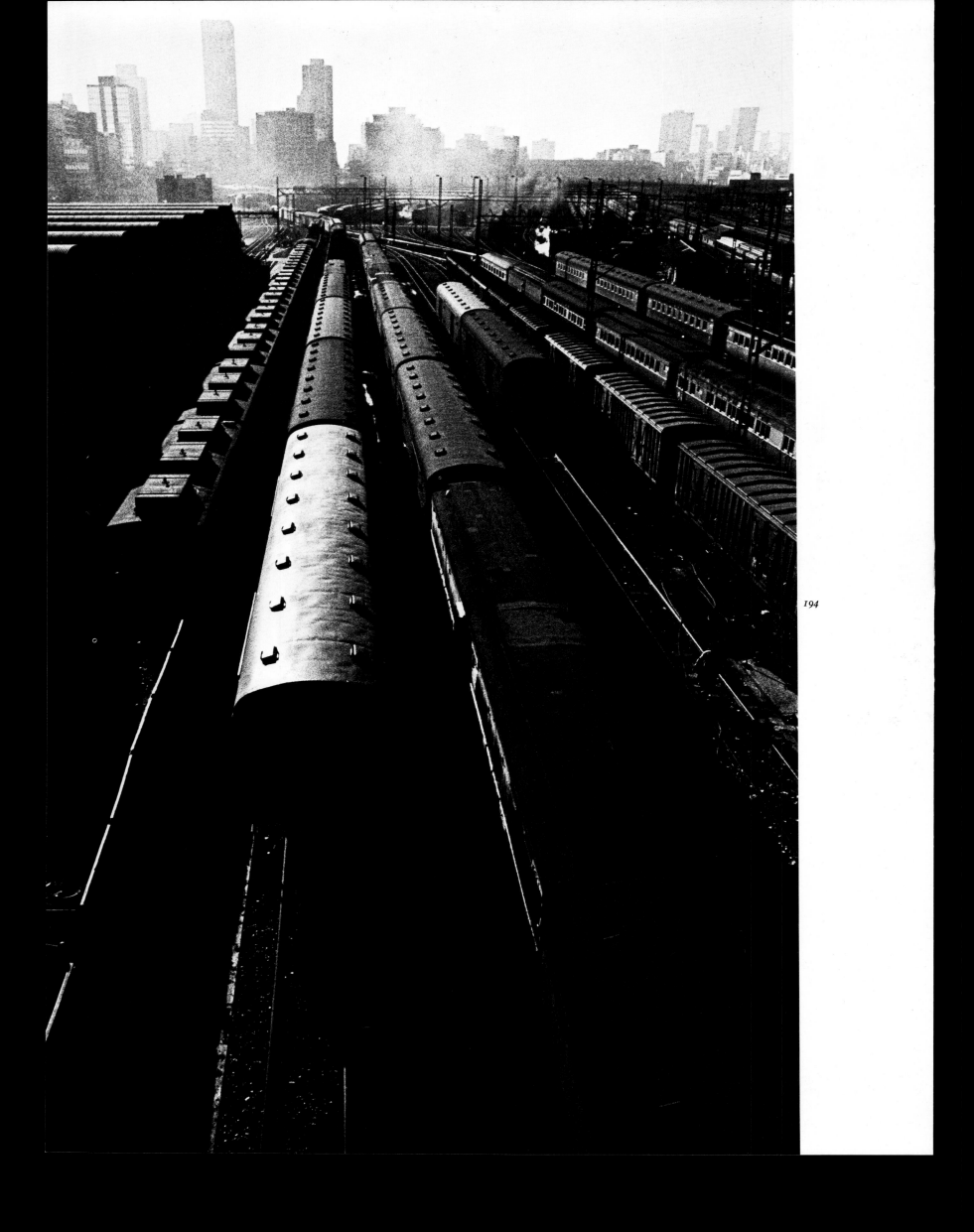

194

195

194, 195. The state-controlled railway, with over 245 000 workers on an annual payroll of R726 million, is the largest single undertaking in South Africa. The four provinces originally managed their railways on a regional basis until Union in 1910 when resources were pooled. The network linked distant dorps (villages) with the towns and cities and encouraged the free flow of goods and passengers throughout the land. Today the S.A.R. & H. (South African Railways and Harbours) has grown to encompass the airlines, oil pipelines and certain areas of manufacture. For enthusiasts, South Africa offers one of the last opportunities in the world to see steam locomotives in regular use, but even with its vast reserves of coal this country cannot afford their high operating costs. At present, about half the 22 million kilometres of railway line in operation are electrified, and eventually the steam locomotive will become a museum piece here too.

196. By road and by rail thousands of commuters enter the city each day from their homes in the urban mass of towns and suburbs of the Rand.

196

197   198

197. *Everybody needs recreational facilities; here Johannesburg's Zoo Lake is the setting.*

198. *What of the future for this city child, no longer secure in the warm embrace of the traditional extended family which was bound by reciprocity and obligation, by a patriarchal system that linked father to brother and cousin to cousin, where each person had a rôle to play and individuality was circumscribed within its bounds? Today, for many urban blacks the immediate family stands alone, dependent on the ability of its individual members to succeed in a competitive society, to hold a job and earn money, to make a home in the overcrowded townships, to find an identity born out of the values of the past and the exigencies of the present.*

199. *City dwellers find common interests to escape Johannesburg's aggressive pace.*

200. *An apprentice herbalist pounds ingredients for a traditional remedy from some of the myriad that festoon this 'muti' shop in Johannesburg. Umuti, traditional medicine, finds a ready market, and belief among black people in its power to cure any* *number of ills – including those attributed to evil spirits – is widespread. An intensive scientific study has revealed that many of the materials used are in fact effective.*

201. *The horseman is no longer a dominant figure in the South African landscape, where his bravado and courage helped shape history, but the products of the craftsman saddler are still in great demand.*

203 204 205

202   206

202. Members of an African Zionist church meet for a baptism by immersion as dawn breaks over the Highveld. The 1970 census reflected that 70% of the black population claimed some Christian affiliation; perhaps the most interesting being some 3 000 African separatist churches with an estimated membership of nearly four million. A synthesis of African and Christian concepts, this movement meets the needs of blacks who accept the broad Christian message but interpret it in their own context, without white participation or domination.

203. By far the majority of the Afrikaans-speaking population belongs to one of the Calvinistic Dutch Reformed churches which exercise a significant influence on their cultural outlook.

204. An Anglican Cathedral in central Pretoria.

205. The ornate interior of a Greek Orthodox Church. In recent years many immigrants have come to settle and there is a thriving Greek community.

206. In a vacant lot a small Zionist group holds a Sunday afternoon service. The all-African churches fall into two categories: those which remain in many ways close to the mission churches from which they seceded, and the Zionists in their bright flowing robes who are very different and have a revivalist, pentecostal flavour.

207. It is predicted that by 1980 there will be six million black children of school-going age in South Africa – equal to the total population in 1900.

208. A leafy lane in suburbia where the city's clamour seems remote.

209. Children at play in the backstreets of Lenasia, an Indian area outside Johannesburg.

210

211

210. The pall of swirling smoke from coal stoves and braziers hangs low over Soweto's neat rows of rectangular houses until well on into the day. The water tower feeds taps, but electricity has yet to reach many of these 'matchbox' houses. Soweto – an acronym for South Western Townships – is not a single township but a vast urban complex in which at least a million people live. From here, in the early dawn each working day, thousands commute to the industrial and commercial centres of the Witwatersrand. The social processes that gave birth to Soweto closely parallel those of the Industrial Revolution in Europe when peasants left the land to seek a new life in the towns. In the last 30 years urbanisation on the Rand has quickened perceptibly and irrevocably. Many children in the townships know no life other than that of the city, yet until Soweto exploded onto the headlines most white South Africans knew little or nothing of its hopes and frustrations. Soweto now confronts South Africa with all the problems that beset the urban black.

211. People of the city.

212 213
     215
214 216

21

212. *Old slimes, residue from the mining process, ravaged by rain and wind. In 1976 the mines milled 76,2 million tonnes of reef (the gold-bearing quartzite), equal to over 12 times the mass of rock in the Great Pyramid of Cheops.*

213. *Before 1912 and the invention of the jackhammer drill, explosive charges were inserted in holes made manually. A quarter of a million workers, mostly migrants from the rural areas or neighbouring black states, go underground each day.*

214. *Gold provided the means and impetus for a modern diversified economy in South Africa. The seven goldfields of the Witwatersrand basin are the focal points for a huge industrial complex that extends over much of the southern Transvaal and northern Orange Free State.*

215. *The muscle of industry has traditionally been black but educated and skilled workers now demand the incentive of access on merit to its higher échelons.*

216. *The mine dancers perform routines that are a fascinating combination of tribal choreography and modern improvisations.*

217. *Shaft sinkers working at depths of over three kilometres below ground-level are the heroes of the workforce. Technology in South Africa has had to overcome seemingly insurmountable problems as the miners follow the narrow seams of gold-bearing ore as it runs ever deeper: heat, pressure and rockbursts are constant dangers but the rewards are high.*

218. *Underground cables are but part of South Africa's sophisticated telecommunications network which must be constantly expanded to keep pace with demand. Even so, more than 50% of the telephones in Africa are installed in the Republic and she is linked by direct dialling to many parts of the world.*

219. *A symbol of technical achievement in South Africa, Sasol is the first and remains the only profitable oil-from-coal project in the world. From this massive plant and a sister scheme will come 40% of the country's petroleum requirements by the 1980s. An alternative source of future energy will be nuclear, drawing raw material from the uranium deposits with which South Africa is so richly endowed.*

220. South Africa has vast reserves of coal, the primary source of her energy. Thermal power-stations have an installed capacity of 15 000 MW – equal to more than half the electricity generated on the entire continent of Africa. The cooling towers in the picture dominate the Eastern Transvaal skyline and such stations, each with turbo-generators of up to 600 MW, supply the base-load for the high-voltage transmission grid that spans the entire country.

221-223. Incandescent metal rolls through a steel mill (221), part of the giant industry that has for the past four decades kept pace with the ever-growing demand for its products. It is virtually self-sufficient in raw materials and only the scarcity of coking coal suitable for metallurgical purposes presents a problem. Costly underground collieries (222) are being augmented by mechanised strip mining but it is the quality of the coal not the quantity that is of vital concern to the steel industry (223).

224. *Bright colours and modern equipment provide a stimulating environment for these school-children.*

225. *Church Square, centre of Pretoria and hub of its public life, was originally a market. Where tar roads and concrete buildings stand today, oxwagons once outspanned. The square was named in honour of the small thatched Dutch Reformed Church consecrated there in 1857, while public buildings erected later along its perimeter trace the growth of Pretoria from country town just over a century ago to administrative capital of South Africa since Union in 1910.*

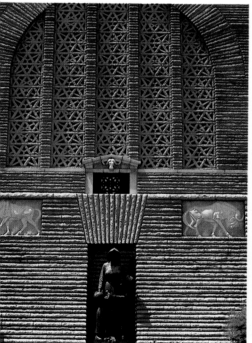

226. A toy train at Pretoria Fountains just outside the city.

227. Pretoria, 70 kilometres north of Johannesburg, is known for the architecture of its buildings, both government and commercial.

228. The city is famous for its tropical jacarandas, here framing the dome and colonnaded façade of the Union Buildings designed by Sir Herbert Baker to commemorate the birth of the Union of South Africa.

229. Overlooking Pretoria is the massive Voortrekker Monument, built by the Afrikaner people to honour the pioneers who trekked north in 1836.

230. One of four bronzes that typify the heroism and defiance of Boer fighters in the 1899-1902 war, at the base of President Paul Kruger's statue in Pretoria. Stephanus Johannes Paulus Kruger, the dedicated leader of the Afrikaners, had as his primary aim unity among his people and the protection of their national integrity.

231. Tribal dress underwent a dramatic change when the European introduced machine-woven cloth to Africa. Before that, Tsonga women dressed themselves in tanned hides. Cross-over drapes conceal voluminously pleated and gathered skirts that today are their 'traditional' dress. As early as the 15th century their ancestors traded ivory, copper, gold and hides for cloth and beads, first with the Arabs and then with the Portuguese at Delagoa Bay in Moçambique.

232. Guests at a Pedi wedding treat it as an occasion to wear their finery that includes abbreviated gathered tops, an adaptation of the maternity smocks introduced by the missionaries long ago. The Pedi fought fiercely against Mzilikazi's Ndebele warriors in 1824. Hendrik Potgieter, who had conquered Mzilikazi, in 1852 led his last commando against the Pedi mountain-stronghold and, although not so well known, tales of Pedi heroism rival those of the more famous Zulu impis.

233. Black babies enjoy a particularly close physical relationship with their mothers who carry them slung on their backs while working or on the move.

233

237

234

236

234. *Along a dusty road, young girls dance and sing songs that are fragments of an oral tradition that reaches far back into their history.*

235. *In this Lowveld valley traditional Tsonga bee-hive huts face the cattle kraal – the ritual centre of the homestead. Within the kraal stands the sacred tree which is closely associated with the ancestor cult universal in the religious beliefs of the black peoples of southern Africa. The traditional relationship between the living and their ancestors is essentially one of propitiation and deference in the belief that the dead take a great interest in the affairs of the mortal world and can affect it. For example, misfortune is still often attributed to the displeasure of the ancestors, and offerings are made in order to regain their favour. Many of these beliefs have lost cogency or been integrated into a broader framework by changing black society.*

236. *The grotesque baobab is perhaps Africa's most famous tree. For the blacks who use the bark and fruit it is a veritable medicine chest, and the trunk, when hollowed out, makes a water tank and granary.*

237. *The dog accompanied the black man on his migrations down Africa and the indigenous species are distinctive – although many have subsequently been cross-bred with imported varieties. Here a young herdsman waits for the end of the day when he and his dog will herd the cattle into the safety of the kraal for the night.*

238. *In this desolate veldscape more than 160 species of grass grow.*

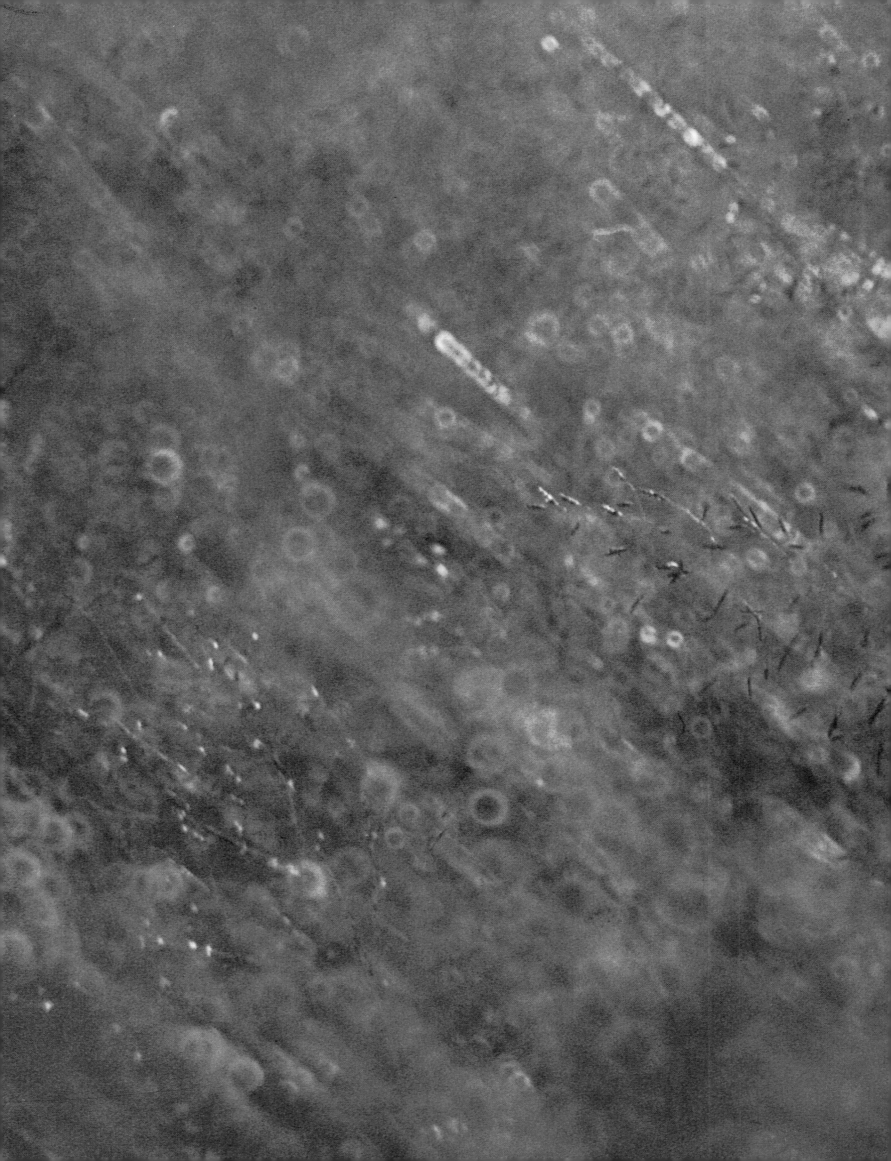

240

239

239. Most stately of the savannah antelopes, the sable (Hippotragus niger) was seen overseas for the first time in 1838 when a specimen reached the British Museum. Most varieties of antelope once abounded in southern Africa, and the early explorers sent back glowing accounts of the wildlife. But indiscriminate hunting, more particularly after the introduction of the rifle, led to a rapid decline in the animal population. One of the first to recognise the threat and suggest that game sanctuaries would provide a solution was President Paul Kruger. The policy of game reserves which he and men such as R. K. Loveday instigated as early as 1884 found its ultimate expression in the reserve that bears his name – the Kruger National Park, largest and most famous in South Africa. From the Crocodile River in the south to the Limpopo in the north, two million hectares of bushveld have been set aside as a sanctuary for a great variety of game; herds have proliferated and the lion reigns as undisputed monarch of this realm.

240. An impala ewe, one of the most numerous species of antelope in the Kruger National Park.

241. Now that the lion is protected from the gun in wildlife sanctuaries he has no natural enemies and can assume his proper rôle at the top of the food chain. With indolence born of power, the pride lazes for much of the time, rousing for the hunt silently and effectively when hungry.

242. A long white-tipped tail, not visible in this picture is the feature that most readily identifies the black wildebeest from the blue. This species roamed South Africa's Highveld in vast numbers until the cattle farmer – and British soldiers with a taste for venison and sport – shot them to the point of extermination at the turn of the century. A few isolated pockets survived and the black wildebeest is now found only in a few wildlife reserves and private game parks.

243. Elephants are matriarchal, an elderly female acting as the dominant member of the group which consists usually of other cows, calves and immature bulls. Mature males either wander alone in the bush or form loosely-knit bachelor herds until mating time when the largest bulls assert their dominance and lay claim to the cows in oestrus.

244

 246 247

245

244. *A baby chacma baboon scratches for fleas. This species was studied intensively by the pioneer naturalist Eugene Marais and by modern students of animal behaviour.*

245. *Brindled gnu or blue wildebeest are animals of the open plains where the lion stalks the young and the sickly. Because predators are a constant threat, mobility is vital and within ten minutes of birth the wildebeest calf can follow its mother and within 24 hours keep up with the galloping herd.*

246. *The diminutive steenbuck depends for survival on its secretive habits for it is preyed upon by large eagles and practically all the carnivorous mammals. Baby steenbuck are concealed in holes until viable and are rarely seen.*

247. *Their sharp eyes alert, these zebra watch for danger. Wildebeest, which have poor sight but an excellent sense of smell, often travel in the company of zebra, the symbiotic relationship ensuring vigilance greater than that which either animal could provide.*

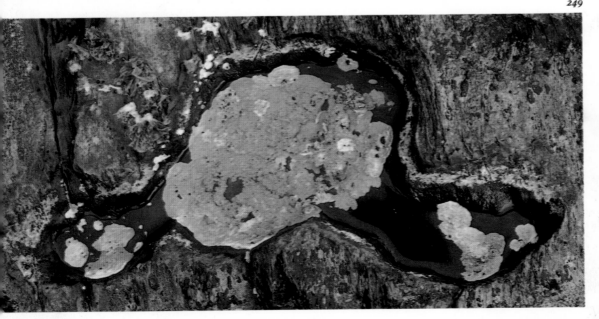

248. *Rivers plunging down the Drakensberg mountains to the Lowveld have eroded magnificent canyons. The forested kloofs and slopes are a palimpsest of geological and human history. To the north, on the Pafuri River are the first rocks that hardened to form the earth's crust. In the black cherts of the Barberton Mountains to the south, fossil algae and bacteria, 3,6 billion years old, hark back to the beginning of life itself. Blacks on their slow migrations south passed through the Lowveld's malarial valleys, and Voortrekkers were stricken with the fever when they brought their wagons down the slopes on the way to the sea. Gold-miners panned the rivers in search of a New Bendigo, and beside the fires of outspanned wagons transport riders spun yarns that were immortalised in* Jock of the Bushveld.

249, 250. *Abstracts of the South African veld.*

250

251

252

251. A small Bushveld farm in what was until recently 'fever country'. A large part of the Eastern Transvaal was the domain of the tsetse fly, so fatal to man and his herds, and the malaria-carrying anopheles mosquito. Early pioneers attempted to destroy the wildlife, itself immune to nagana (trypanosomiasis) but a vector which spreads the disease to cattle. Against the mosquito, quinine and claustrophobic screened houses were the only defence until the final conquest of the forbidding Bushveld began 40 years ago in the research laboratories of preventive medicine. Today cattle ranching is the main activity.

252. Pebbles scoured these pot-holes which once held nuggets that by 1874 had lured more than 1 500 diggers to this area. Many rivers of the Lowveld yielded gold from their gravels and Bourke's Luck, shown here, was the site of a 'big find'. The Pilgrim's Rest goldfield at the head of the Blyde River yielded £1 500 000 worth in four years.

253. The 56-metres high Mac-Mac Falls on the Waterval River. The name recalls the visit of President Burgers of the Transvaal to a goldfield where there were so many Scotsmen among the diggers that he called it 'Mac-Mac'. Diggers the world over came to take part in South Africa's first gold rush.

254

255

256

257

258

254. Here on the still peaceful Tugela estuary on the east coast there are plans for an industrial complex which may one day rival the Witwatersrand.

255. Along the Natal coast, beautiful river mouths such as this one are nurseries for marine life and therefore need protection.

256. Future playground of South Africa, the still unspoilt Indian Ocean coastline.

257. Land plants that grow closest to the sea, these Scaevola thunbergii are named after the father of South African botany, the Swede, Carl Thunberg.

258. Surf fishermen at Sordwana Bay.

259
261

260
262

263

259. *The many-hued 'barber's shop shrimp'* (Stenopus hispidus), *one of the prizes gathered from a mudflat on the Natal coast.*

260. *No single organism, but a veritable colony in which each constituent has a separate function, the bluebottle or Portuguese man-o'-war floats with the current.*

261. *A featherstar* (Crinoidia) *opens its arms to form the 'begging bowl' into which the organic matter on which it feeds will fall.*

262. *Horny coral, like the sea anemone, extends tentacles, armed with stinging cells into which small marine organisms swim and are paralysed.*

263. *Underwater blossoms transform Natal's coastline into a submarine garden.*

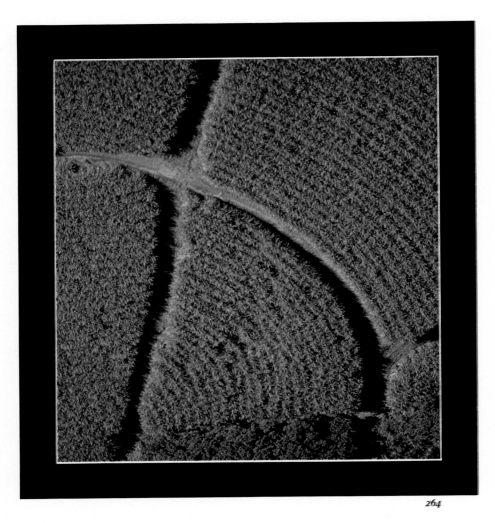

264

265

264. *The ordered pattern of sugarcane fields seen from the air. For almost 400 kilometres along Natal's green coast the indigenous forest has been cleared to make way for the cane which was introduced to this country in 1848 and which is now the basis of an industry that produces two million tonnes of sugar a year. The Zulu cultivated a sweet sorghum, called imphi, which they crushed between stones to extract the juice, but the cane on which industry is based came from Réunion.*

265. *The ox-drawn sled is still a familiar sight in Natal's rural areas where many black farmers work smallholdings allocated to the heads of families by the chiefs. Inherent in this system is the assumption that land is amply available for allocation. This is no longer so, and although Natal is fertile and well-watered, traditional farming methods cannot provide sufficient food to meet the demands of the rapidly growing black population. Experts believe that only consolidation of individual holdings will result in efficient agriculture. But tradition dies hard.*

266

267

268

269

266. *Christian religious communities often cluster round small churches that stand seemingly isolated on mission reserves. Missionaries were among the first to study 'Bantu' spoken in many interrelated but different forms by the African peoples south of the Equator. Initially students in this field simply collected lists of words, but they were not first to make such written record; as early as 2 500 BC the Egyptians recorded the word Bantu, probably referring to the land of the 'Bantu'. However, a systematic study was only begun in the mid-17th century, notably by a man of the church. Since then many such men have contributed significantly to the development of an orthography and grammar for the various Bantu languages and dialects found in southern Africa.*

267. *These cheerful lads belong to one of the nine broad groupings of black people in South Africa. Zulu and Xhosa, with five million people each, are the largest; others of importance are the Swazi, Ndebele, South Sotho, Tswana, Pedi, Tsonga and Venda.*

268. *For months these Venda girls will be kept in isolation, their days given over to dancing, sex instruction and manual work.*

269. *Buses link rural areas with urban townships.*

270. Probably no black person in South Africa today remains unaffected by the impact of Western culture and technology. Even here, in the sanctuary of her hut in an isolated rural area, this Zulu woman's life reflects fundamental change. Her husband is in a distant town and his earnings provide the possessions that clutter her hut. The portable radio receives broadcasts in her own language and introduces ideas of the outside world that encompass things as divergent as savings banks and washing powders, tinned foods and pension schemes. The bicycle is an innovation; so, too, are the enamel pots in place of ones that her mother knew how to make of clay. The kitten is something the European brought to Africa as well. Yet not everything in her life has changed, even though by the time the child still at the breast grows up, many of the traditions she still clings to will be but memories. And dress, no less than expectations, will

reflect the new reality. Even today fewer women are still wearing this traditional hairstyle made by working the stretched and ochred strands of hair over a wooden frame, and the black leather skirt, traditional Zulu symbol of marriage, is now rarely seen.

271. Much has altered during this old Zulu's lifetime; yet the Zulu were themselves the instruments of far-reaching change in southern Africa during the 18th and 19th centuries. Under a succession of powerful and often inspired autocrats, the loose social groupings of Nguni people in what was to become Natal, were forged into a powerful kingdom of warriors feared throughout the land. Prior to the emergence of leaders such as Dingiswayo, Shaka and Dingane, the social system of the Zulu, like that of most of the other Bantu-speaking peoples, was one of loosely related clans linked by allegiances to various

chiefs, and interrelated by marriage. But among the Zulu it was transformed by three brilliant innovations: firstly, the reorganisation of the army along lines of age that cut across old allegiances with each age-group regiment swearing fealty to the king alone; secondly, the introduction of the short stabbing-assegai in place of the traditional throwing spear; and lastly the superb military training and discipline of the warriors which forged the Zulu into a formidable fighting machine without peer on the southern continent. Their rampages brought terror and bloodshed, the strong fled and the weak were conquered. With their disastrous defeat at Isandhlwana the British, too, discovered that they were a force to be reckoned with. Britain eventually defeated them, but the memory of power remains strong and the Zulu retain their identity and their spirit.

272. *The harbour city of the Green Coast, Durban has grown fat and rich from the ships that use the port, the canefields that spread over the hills, and the plateau people inland who come to holiday on its beaches. The history of its birth and pioneering youth is a tale of African adventure that began in the 1820s when George Francis Farewell and his companion ventured into the interior in search of ivory. They* *were witness to Shaka's military onslaughts on the Pondo and they traded with the wily king and eventually won his trust. Their small huts on the shores of Durban Bay marked the birth of the city which has now become the biggest port in Africa. It handles more than half the exports and imports of the Republic and has become a major industrial city.*

273. *The city of Durban, a tropical metropolis where much of the business is essentially mixed with pleasure.*

274

275

27

274. More than a quarter of a million people visit Durban each year and the hotels, many of which crowd the Golden Mile along the beachfront, have 32 000 beds available at any given time. The warm surf and tropical sunshine are great attractions to people who live at high inland altitudes and regard a yearly descent to sea-level as essential to their health, making Durban the Blackpool of the Indian Ocean.

275. Slumbering hotel guests rarely see the Indian fishermen as they launch their craft before sunrise. Erosion of rivers and lagoons which were the spawning ground of many fish species, has made the catches grow smaller year by year.

276. Charming visitors to Durban's beachfront mecca can bathe safely behind the barrier of knitted nets protecting popular swimming places from the shark waters, not only in Durban, but at the numerous holiday resorts along the coast. Twenty years ago a series of attacks was followed by a mass exit of holidaymakers and the resorts of the South Coast became ghost towns until effective measures were introduced. Today tourism is a major source of income in Natal.

277. *Each year in midwinter immense shoals of pilchards travel along the Natal coast, their final destination unknown. And close behind the so-called 'sardine run' come the predators, game fish that provide sport for fishermen.*

278. *Set in the rolling countryside of the Umhlatuzana River valley on the outskirts of Durban is Chatsworth, an Indian township designed to house ultimately some 200 000 people.*

277

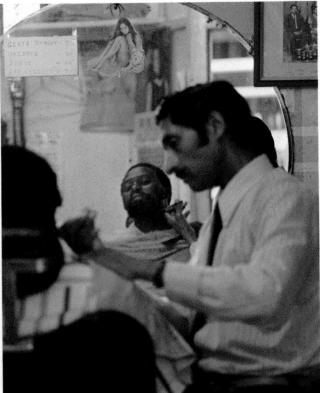

279

280 281

282

279. Durban has the largest Indian population of any city outside India. These girls in a city park wear Western dress, but the graceful sweep of a sari is seen just as often.

280. With a Hindu temple as her backdrop, a young Indian girl performs the stylised movements of a dance steeped in ancient religious tradition.

281. A Zulu customer receives a beard trim at an Indian barbershop.

282. A Hindu couple, garlanded with flowers, are married in the groom's home according to custom. Equivalent of the wedding ring will be the vermilion kutum on the bride's forehead.

283. This Indian merchant practises a trade as old as the spice routes. In his jars there are ground ginger, cinnamon bark, flower buds of the clove tree, coriander and dill, turmeric, nutmeg and neem patta *curry leaves*: spices for the dishes that the Indians brought with them to Natal when they came in the 1860s as indentured labourers for the sugar industry which could not induce Zulu men, secure in their traditional economy, to do 'women's work' in the fields. Thousands of Indians were brought out under the scheme and all had free tickets back to India after five years, but most exchanged them for smallholdings and chose to make Natal their new home. Others came out as 'free passengers' who paid their own way. Several plans to repatriate the Indians were made, but after a century they can no longer be regarded as temporary sojourners and are accepted as Indian South Africans. Four-fifths of South Africa's 620 000 Indians live in Natal and make a significant contribution to the economy at every level.

284. Within the term 'Indian South African' is hidden a tremendous diversity of cultures, languages and religious beliefs. But for most Indians the extended family is still a powerful force and young girls like these are chaperoned until marriage when a woman is expected to go and live with her husband's family and come under the authority of her mother-in-law.

284

285

286

287

283

285. For this little boy in festive dress, a good education and professional training will have high priority.

286. Most Indians in Natal are Hindu and the temple of which this statue is part is the oldest in South Africa.

287. An old Hindu woman tends the household shrine.

288

289

288. Inland from the Green Coast lie the foothills of the Drakensberg where regular winter snow gleams briefly on the slopes. Here, in the sheep and dairy country of Griqualand East, a sad postscript to the history of the Hottentots was written. The Griquas, who were largely Hottentot with an admixture of Bushman, white and black blood, were proudly independent. From their first settlement south of the confluence of the Vaal and Orange Rivers they rode forays against Mantatee and Matabele impis who were no match for these mounted commandos armed with guns. Able chiefs like Adam Kok and Andries Waterboer accepted missionaries and learnt to irrigate wheat. As British subjects they refused to send recruits to the Cape Regiment and in 1869 they were removed to the Drakensberg foothills in the east where they eventually lost their land, bit by bit, and moved to the towns where their identity became one with the coloureds.

289. The sangoma (diviner) fulfils an important function in traditional belief where spirits and witchcraft are often blamed for misfortune.

290. The tree of knowledge spreads its branches faster than the roofs of classrooms. Here a teacher and her pupils gather outside their school in the wintery foothills of the Drakensberg.

290

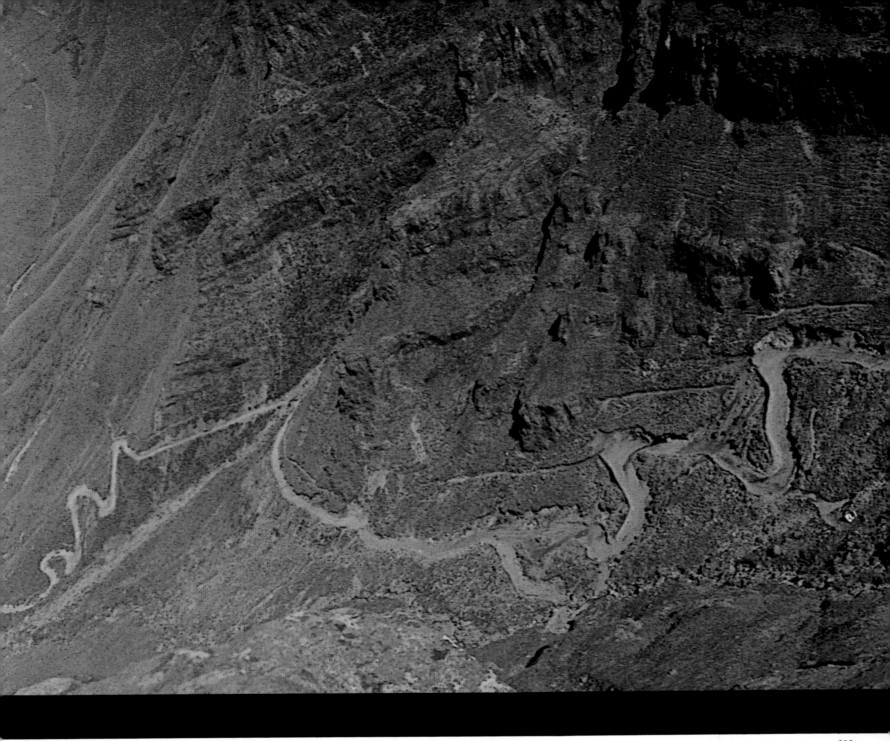

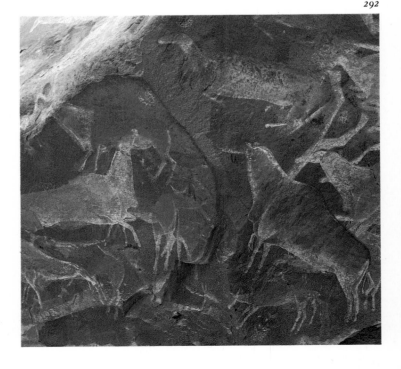

291. The Sani Pass, twisted brown ribbon of a dirt road over the Dragon Mountain – the Drakensberg – is famous for its bends and gradients that challenge even the modern motor-car. The original 20 kilometres, which only the sturdy Basuto pony could tackle, was widened in 1958 so that jeeps could roar to the top of the 2 877 metre high pass and the Lesotho border post. But progress has come to the peaks. About 70 kilometres further on there is the diamond mine at Letsieng-la-Terai and further still is the site of the Oxbow Dam, a project that could help to slake the Witwatersrand's growing thirst.

292. The Bushman artists of the Drakensberg painted the stately eland with such precision that the click of hooves seems to reverberate on the rockface. The rock painting of the Drakensberg is relatively recent compared with that of the hunter-artists of southern France and Spain – or even with Bushman art in other parts of southern Africa. Yet this lends it special interest for these Stone Age artists were at work in historic times. They have left their record of the coming of the Zulu and of the trekkers' wagons and soldiers who would eventually drive them from their mountain strongholds.

293

295

294

293. *A view over the Drakensberg, the outstanding feature of South Africa's physiography – a mountainous spine over 1 000 kilometres in length running almost parallel to the east coast. It marks the edge of the inland plateau and presents a barrier between the plains of the interior and the eastern coastlands.*

294. *Many rivers have scoured tortuous paths into the Drakensberg's basalt.*

295. *High above the nests of the Black Eagle and Lammergeyer, man soars with a frail glider over the Drakensberg.*

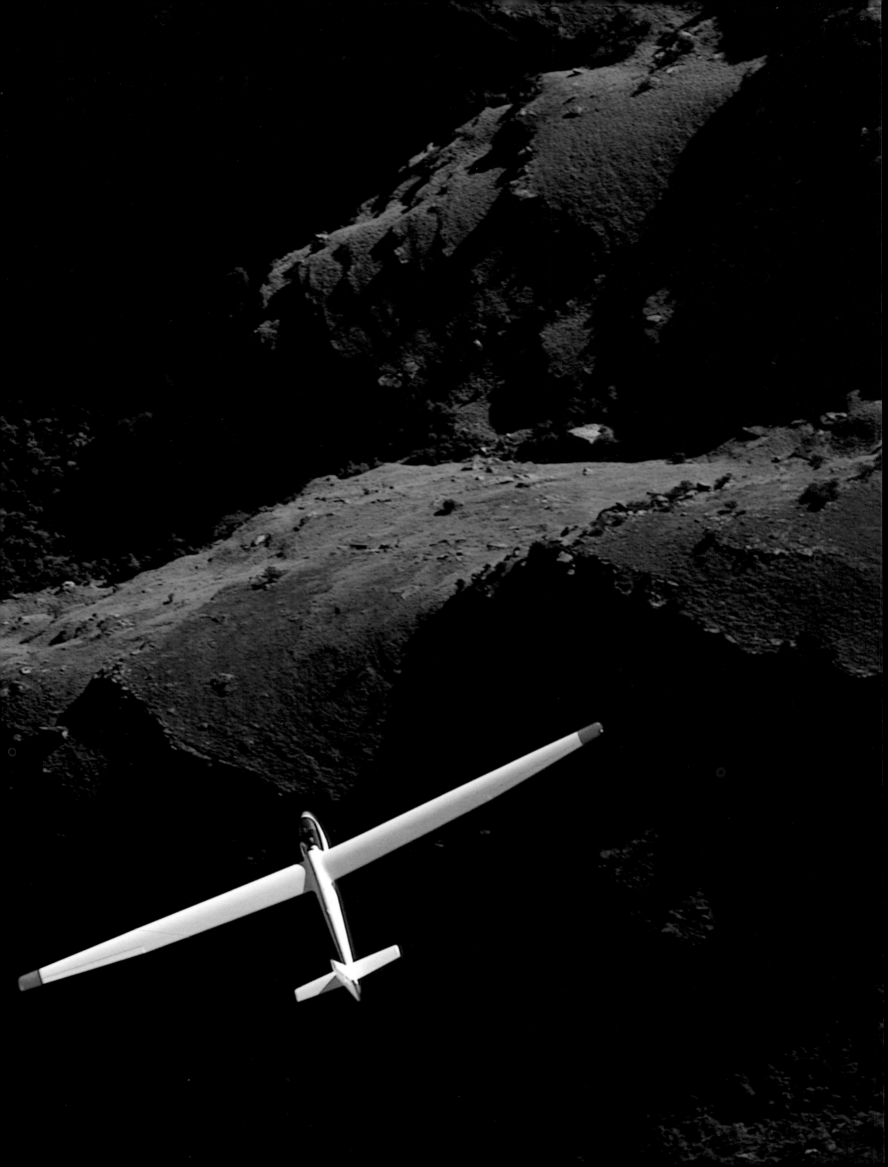

296

297

296. A storm gathers over the Amphitheatre in the Drakensberg's Royal Natal National Park. The Voortrekkers, weary from their long trek across the Highveld, stood at the edge of the escarpment and looked down on a scene so beautiful that they called it 'the Promised Land'.

297. The Devil's Tooth, a spire of rock, that for years defied man's onslaughts.

Photographers